ABOUT THE AUTHOR

G ary Burnison is a *New York Times* best-selling author and CEO of Korn Ferry, a global organizational consulting firm. He is the author of eight previous leadership and career advancement books, including *Lose the Resume, Land the Job*, which The New York Times Book Review said, "breaks down every aspect of job hunting, explaining what matters and what doesn't." His most recent book is *The 5 Graces of Life and Leadership*. Gary is a CNBC contributor and is regularly featured in major media. He is all about helping others exceed their potential.

Published by John Wiley & Sons, Inc., Hoboken, New Jersey.

Published simultaneously in Canada.

For general information on our other products and services or for technical support, please contact our Customer Care Department within the United States at (800) 762-2974, outside the United States at (317) 572-3993 or fax (317) 572-4002.

Wiley also publishes its books in a variety of electronic formats. Some content that appears in print may not be available in electronic formats. For more information about Wiley products, visit our web site at www.wiley.com.

Library of Congress Cataloging-in-Publication Data is Available:
ISBN: 9781394150052 (paperback)
ISBN: 9781394150069 (ePub)
ISBN: 9781394150076 (ePDF)

Cover Design and Images: Courtesy of Jonathan Pink, Hayley Kennell, Tim Ames

Author Photo: Peter Figen Photography

SKY10034993_082622

TAKE CONTROL

THE CAREER YOU WANT, WHERE YOU WANT

Gary Burnison

TAKE CONTROL

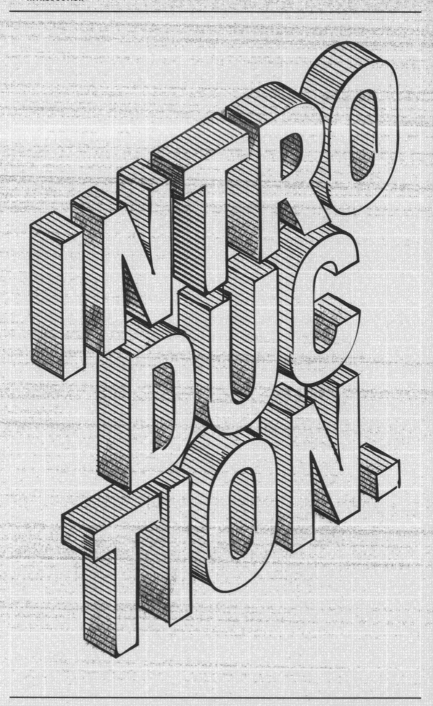

INTRODUCTION

"I want to work from Tahiti."

This wasn't the opening line I had expected when I sat down to talk with the daughter of a friend, who had asked for my advice as she prepared to enter the workforce.

When I asked where she wanted to work, I thought we would be discussing what industries or companies might be a good fit, based on her solid experience, including internships at household brand organizations. Maybe, at the end of our conversation, she'd ask me to take a look at her resume and provide some feedback.

Instead, she began mentioning places around the world where she personally wanted to live with the assumption that she could work anywhere—and the opportunities would follow. "Madrid would be another option. Or Cozumel. What do you think?"

At first, I wanted to laugh, as if she were kidding. But maybe the joke was on me. Am I the dinosaur or is this what everyone is thinking?

As mind-boggling as this conversation was, it does reflect the dramatic transformation of the past few years, including today's work anytime, from anywhere reality. And it cuts across all generations and demographics.

The workscape has changed. Think about it. Everything we experienced in the past has been turned on its head—how we produce, how we consume, how we're entertained, how we travel for business ... and more. For so many people just starting their careers, working virtually and this environment are all they know. And, for everyone else who has had the remote option, work is no longer synonymous with a physical location.

FOR SO MANY PEOPLE JUST STARTING THEIR CAREERS, WORKING VIRTUALLY AND THIS ENVIRONMENT ARE ALL THEY KNOW

It's a push-pull world, and you have to be able to navigate and negotiate between the flexibility and opportunity you want—and the commitment and performance that organizations need. In other words, you should know how to take control.

If two years ago, someone had described the metaverse, would we have believed it? Would we have embraced it? How about hiring people we've never met in person? Working anywhere—from a kitchen table to a cafe? Leaving your workplace in March 2020—never to return again, while maybe being more efficient in your job? Sound plausible? I can remember in the old world flying overnight from Los Angeles to Germany, going directly to a meeting, and immediately flying home again. Now, I can accomplish the same thing with an hour of Zoom. And that's here to stay.

This book is all about that reality, and it applies to your entire career lifecycle—whether you're just starting out or you've been at this for several years or for decades and are now struggling to adapt to this new environment. Whether you're focused on getting your next job or you are striving to get ahead where you are. And, whether your ideal is going into an office or working remotely— or some fluid and ambiguous combination of both (depending on the day).

Over the past few years, I've engaged in countless conversations and discussions with executives and professionals. All ages, phases, and levels of experience.

With more seasoned executives, a question I often ask (and I've pondered it myself, too) is to imagine that they were starting over in their career—and in today's environment. Would they have advanced to the level where they are now? Would they have to do things differently?

Almost to a person, they all needed to pause and reflect. Most confided to me that they were not sure where they would have ended up. But, after giving it some thought, everyone said that yes, they'd absolutely have to do things differently to get ahead in today's new reality compared to yesterday's world.

And that's what this book offers—not only the perspective of someone who has been CEO of a publicly traded company for more than 15 years, but also the insights from the firm that develops 1 million professionals a year and places someone in a job every three minutes of the workday. The advice here is drawn from assessments of more than 86 million professionals (so we know what "great" looks like). And we're constantly coaching, developing, and advancing professionals, at all levels of organizations.

Based on what we're hearing, and everywhere we look, the workscape is more complex. But it's also more adaptable than you may realize. And you have to be, too—especially looking ahead to when the job market tightens and the pendulum swings from what people want toward what organizations need. Even so, with learning agility and self-awareness, there will always be a way.

Like the professional who had asked me for some advice on whether or not to pursue a job with a very well-known tech company (you'd recognize the name, believe me). This company is known for creating an ecosystem for its employees—an immersive world of working, eating, and even exercising onsite. What were once viewed just a few years ago as highly desirable perks, though, are now sometimes seen as drawbacks—at least for some people. As this person told me, "If I work for them, they'd expect me to spend *so much time* there."

"But what if that weren't the case?" I asked. "What if you could ask for—and get—the flexibility you wanted?"

The pause that followed told me this person had not really considered this possibility before. Rather, the assumption was that things were set in stone for that employer—and that's simply not what I'm hearing these days.

> # NOW AND IN THE FUTURE, THE WORKSCAPE IS NOT *EITHER/OR*. IT'S ALL ABOUT THE *AND*. AS PAST CYCLES HAVE SHOWN, THE PENDULUM SWINGS IN BOTH DIRECTIONS

When it comes to how work gets done—now and in the future—it's not *either/or*. It's all about the *and*.

And don't think this applies only to Millennials and Gen Z. I've heard plenty of seasoned professionals and even senior executives say they don't miss their daily commutes of two-hours-plus (sometimes each way). After working from home for two years, they can't imagine going back to an office every day.

If that sounds like you, you're in good company. In one recent survey, more than 80% of the people who have been working from home say they don't want to go back into the office or prefer some hybrid arrangements (which is code for not going into the office very much). Other surveys indicate that some people not only want (and need) to continue working remotely, but some of them might even quit if their employers aren't flexible.

BUT THAT'S CERTAINLY NOT EVERYBODY. ONE COLLEAGUE TOLD ME THAT SHE'S EXCITED TO BE BACK IN THE OFFICE

But that's certainly not everybody. One colleague told me that she's excited to be back in the office. Not only does that fit her personal life, but it also meshes with her responsibilities. As we talked, she confided another reason: "I miss seeing people in person." Turns out, those happenstance conversations—in the office kitchen while getting coffee, in the hallway—were a big part of the ties that connect us. We miss them and need to find a way to replicate them in a work-anywhere environment. And so goes today's topsy-turvy workscape.

Then there was the mid-20s college graduate in his second full-time job. Throughout our conversation he kept bragging to me about the "office culture" where he worked. But, come to find out, he wasn't actually

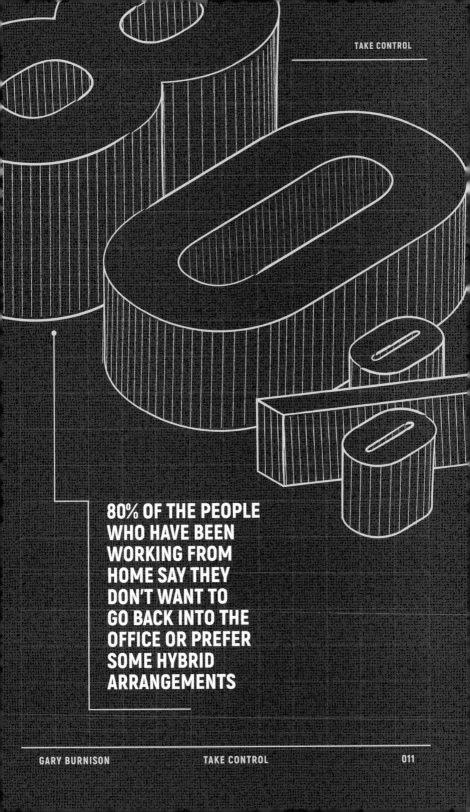

80% OF THE PEOPLE WHO HAVE BEEN WORKING FROM HOME SAY THEY DON'T WANT TO GO BACK INTO THE OFFICE OR PREFER SOME HYBRID ARRANGEMENTS

working in-person—and neither were most people in the company. The more he hyped his office culture, it occurred to me that his Zoom-based world didn't depend on an office to have a culture.

The bottom line: In this new world, it's not about where you work. And that's true if you never go into a physical location, or you are in a profession that requires you to be onsite every day. Today, more than ever, it's all about the *why*—as in, why you do what you do.

—

TAKE THE BEST, LEAVE THE REST

To be honest, my own thinking on this has evolved. Much earlier in my career, when I worked with a West Coast investment bank, I noticed that the CEO looked a little bit disheveled by mid-afternoon. Then I discovered that the CEO routinely came into the office at four o'clock in the morning, and sometimes after his daily jog. He was there two-and-a-half-hours before the stock market opened so he could monitor overseas markets—and, frankly, that was just the way he liked to operate.

This example stayed with me. When I first joined Korn Ferry, I made it a habit to be in the office by six or six-thirty each morning. But now, my thinking has gone

180 degrees. It is possible to be committed—or as I call it, all-in, all the time—without being physically present. After all, it's not activity that matters most—it's about achievement.

NO MORE APPLYING YESTERDAY'S MINDSET TO TODAY'S REALITY. WE TAKE THE BEST—AND LEAVE THE REST

No more applying yesterday's mindset to today's reality. We take the best—and leave the rest.

Think back to when we were in school. The day sometimes started in homeroom, where everybody had to be at a desk for attendance. Ironically, though, it was a positive experience back then and for one important reason: Homeroom wasn't a class—it was a "horizontal community" of students who often were not in classes together the rest of the day.

Today, we're seeing more "horizontal homerooms" within organizations, so that community and opportunity are omnipresent and available to everyone, no matter where or how people work. There is no one-size-fits-all solution that applies to every organization or even within an organization.

The center of gravity is shifting—from a place of work to a location for collaboration. It's headspace and heart space. And within that mix, agility is critical to your success.

—

WHAT'S YOUR WHY?

FROM A JOB TO *THE JOB*

This has been the hottest job market we've ever seen. Getting a job isn't a problem for many people. But getting *the job*—where you're happy and motivated, and more likely to outperform—well, that's another story.

A friend of mine called me the other day, wanting to discuss his 27-year-old daughter who had just changed full-time jobs for the fourth time in five years. Just two weeks into her latest job, she was interviewing with yet another company. Like so many career nomads—moving from job to job after only a year or two (and sometimes after far less time than that)—she was tempted to make another leap.

I get it. The days of approaching a career path as a ladder—moving slowly and steadily upwards, eyes on where you want to be in 10 years—are over. Today, the focus is much, much shorter. As a result, career paths are more like labyrinths, looping around before moving ahead. And "job-hopping' is no longer the pejorative it used to be, especially these days. But that doesn't change the fact that the best reason to make a job change is to move toward something—not just run away.

With that advice in mind, I agreed to call my friend's daughter. The first question I asked was why she was changing jobs so soon. "Because I could," she replied, half-joking. But *could* does not automatically translate into *should*. So, I asked her, "What's your why?"

She paused. "My what?" Now, we were getting somewhere.

"Your why is your purpose, your intrinsic motivator—the reason for making this decision," I explained.

Then she let down her guard and proceeded to give me a window into her why: remote everything, every day feels the same, disconnected, missing being with people... She wanted to change jobs for the simple fact that she hoped to land somewhere—anywhere—different.

But at two weeks into her job, there was still so much she could do where she was: connect with coworkers, network across the company, learn all she could, and help shape— not just adapt to—the culture.

In other words, instead of escaping after 14 days, she could be part of the solution. If after six months she still felt that the job was a bad fit, then she could move on. But at least she'd know more about herself and her why—and that would get her closer to the right job to advance her career.

—

NO SHORTCUTS
TO SUCCESS

Instead of merely moving from job to job, without a real plan, it's time to consider where you really want to be. But that does take some effort. The sad fact is that people still spend more time doing research when buying a flat-screen TV or a washing machine than thinking about how to get ahead in their careers.

Consider the fact that over the course of a lifetime, the average person spends:

- 10,625 days looking at a digital device.
- 7,709 days sitting down.
- 1,769 days socializing.
- 240 days laughing.
- 180 days exercising.

Yet, they spend too little time thinking about how to advance their careers. It's time to take control—with purpose and positivity. And that's where this book comes in.

The goal here is to have not only the right job, but also the right career—the one that makes you feel that you really are connected to something bigger than yourself. It's purpose and passion, combined. And, yes, you can have that.

10,625 DAYS
**LOOKING AT A
DIGITAL DEVICE**

7,709 DAYS
SITTING DOWN

1,769 DAYS
SOCIALIZING

240 DAYS
LAUGHING

180 DAYS
EXERCISING

As a CEO, I can tell you that companies are looking for people who equate their work with the pursuit of meaning—their life goals and destination. You can be one of them, and my hope is that this book will be the guide to help get you there.

This book charts your career path in three sections:

The first is
- **HOW YOU'RE WIRED**

You'll understand the importance of your A.C.T.—being **authentic**, making a **connection**, and giving others a **taste** of who you are. You'll explore the importance of tapping your right brain—and why learning it all is the secret to sustainable success.

The second is
- **HOW TO GET THE JOB—AND GET AHEAD**

There's a big difference between getting a job and *the* job—and that's what this section is all about: targeting your next opportunity, networking to get an introduction, and nailing the interview.

The third is
· HOW TO WORK WITH OTHERS

Now that you have the job you want, it's time to turn your sights to how to advance your career. That includes mastering the 4 Career Knockout Punches, getting along with your boss and coworkers, navigating culture, and communicating and connecting.

This is the new norm. Instead of asking why—it's time to ask, "why not!" You can have the career you've always wanted and deserve—that is, if you're willing to take control.

—

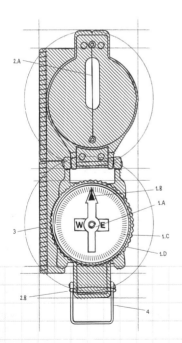

AS A CEO, I CAN TELL YOU THAT COMPANIES ARE LOOKING FOR PEOPLE WHO EQUATE THEIR WORK WITH THE PURSUIT OF MEANING

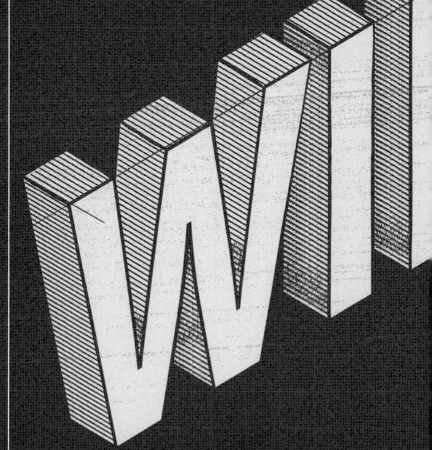

RED

HOW
YOU'RE
WIRED

TAKE CONTROL

Chapter 1

YOUR OPENING A.C.T.

What matters most is the story you tell—conveying not only what you can do but, as important, who you are. It's about your A.C.T.:

- **AUTHENTIC**
  Truthfully presenting yourself
  and your experience

- **CONNECTION**
  Forging a positive emotional
  connection with others

- **TASTE**
  Giving people a "taste" of
  who you are

A.C.T. is a mindset, a language. It shapes every conversation and interaction—whether you're networking, interviewing, navigating a new world of work, meeting people in the office or by remote. A.C.T. establishes rapport and relatability.

Many years ago, when I was starting out in my career, someone in my network introduced me to a hiring manager at a company I wanted to work for. When the manager invited me to send a copy of my resume, I spent countless hours writing, rewriting, and polishing it. I wanted my resume to be perfect.

When it came time for the in-person interview, the hiring manager opened our conversation with the usual icebreaker: "So, tell me about yourself."

Immediately, I began reciting the positions I'd held thus far. The manager interrupted me. "I know what's on your resume. Tell me about you. Tell me a story so I can really know who you are."

This experience changed my career path—and probably my life. I got the job, and all because I grasped two important truths:

The first is a resume is not the gateway to a new job (let alone the right job). Unfortunately, many people still think their resume accounts for 90 percent of what it takes to get a new job, when actually it's only about 10 percent. The second is always be your authentic self.

—

WHO ARE YOU...
REALLY?

I f the past few years have taught us anything, it's the power of being authentic. We go beyond the superficiality of what we do and become vulnerable enough to show others *who we are*—by sharing some of the defining moments of our lives.

When I was ten years old, I had a moment that shaped me forever. I can still remember: It was a cold day, about two-thirty in the afternoon, and outside it was pouring rain. A huge truck pulled up in front of our house; its back doors swung open, and the ramp was brought down. As two men approached our house, I looked past them to the truck and wondered: Were we moving?

WHEN MY DAD CAME UP BESIDE ME, THERE WERE TEARS IN HIS EYES. HE SAID, "SON, IT WILL BE OK."

When my dad came up beside me, there were tears in his eyes. He said, "Son, it will be OK." Then I watched as all our furniture was carried out the front door. My father had gone bankrupt, and everything was repossessed.

That moment defined my work ethic and drive to succeed—but it did something else, as well. Over the years, whenever I share my personal story, it always amazes me how people immediately respond with their own stories. It never fails to happen. We all have our backgrounds and experiences that become the legacy we carry forward on our journey. The more we open up and share, the more authentic we become and the more relatable we are to others.

> **WE EACH KNEW WHAT IT WAS LIKE TO WALK IN EACH OTHER'S SHOES. AND THIS IS HOW OUR A.C.T. BECOMES THE FOUNDATION OF OUR EMPATHY**

Once in a client meeting—during the "where did you grow up" smalltalk—I shared a story about being embarrassed as a high school student to go with my dad to the grocery store because we had to pay with food stamps. "I had a very similar experience," a top executive of the other company told me. When we locked eyes, we each knew what it was like to walk in each other's shoes. And this is how our A.C.T. becomes the foundation of our empathy.

—

LYIN' LARRY

And then there was Larry—the polar opposite.

FROM AUTHENTICITY TO EMPATHY

Empathy is all about meeting others where they are—to understand who they are. To show empathy, though, we first must possess it—and that comes from being authentic.

We know that people are not all the same, nor are they in the same place. But with empathy and compassion, we can meet them wherever they are and provide them with what they truly need.

Empathy broadcasts, verbally and nonverbally, "I know how you feel. Our circumstances may be different, but I've been there, too." It can become the catalyst that turns "we're all in this together" from only words to a feeling and then to an action.

It's during these times that we start down a path. Often, it begins with "cognitive empathy," of merely trying to walk in someone else's shoes. It progresses to sympathy, that "emotional empathy" when we try to feel what another person is experiencing. At last, we reach "empathetic care," an action that manifests as care and genuine concern for others.

EMPATHY BROADCASTS, VERBALLY AND NONVERBALLY

OH, THAT'S LARRY BEING LARRY

This was someone I knew many years ago. The guy was brilliant and could discuss any subject—current events, politics, history, sports—with remarkable depth and insight. And when it came to job performance, Larry was amazing. But Larry wielded his intelligence like a weapon. Although I wouldn't be surprised if he had an IQ of 150, Larry was completely lacking in emotional intelligence and people skills.

Larry decided he didn't have to follow the rules that applied to everyone else. He routinely blew off meetings and, when he did show up, he talked over people, crushed anyone who disagreed with him, and was completely uninterested in anything anyone else had to say. After waltzing into a meeting late, Larry thought nothing of flipping through a magazine while his colleagues made presentations or discussed their latest wins.

Larry was also tough to pin down on anything, from where he was to what he was doing. (Not long ago, I interviewed someone who I thought probably knew Larry. When I inquired, the person replied, "Oh, of course I know him. The thing about Larry is he only lies when his lips are moving.")

His performance was so stellar, though, people made excuses for him: "Oh, that's Larry being Larry." Over time, Larry's arrogance, intellectual superiority, and downright rudeness became highly toxic to the group. Let's just say he got voted off the island. Losing his performance was hard but making the decision to ask him to leave was easy.

Most of us have a little bit of "Larryness" in us—but usually it's just trying to pass ourselves off as something that we're not. It may seem harmless at the time— trying to put ourselves in a better light or maybe avoiding embarrassment. But the truth is we're hiding a part of what helps define who we are.

BUT THE TRUTH IS WE'RE HIDING A PART OF WHAT HELPS DEFINE WHO WE ARE

I experienced this when I was a young teenager. After basketball practice, as the other kids waited outside the gym doors for their parents to pick them up, I started walking in the other direction—telling my teammates I had someplace else to be.

The truth, though, was I always asked my dad to meet me a few blocks away. It was the early 1970s, and I didn't want anyone to see my dad's car—a 1956 Buick with a rusted bumper that belched blue clouds of exhaust. As I slunk low in the seat of that car, my dad knew what was going on—and I knew that he knew. But we never talked about it. He just let me be.

Today, of course, I'd love to have that old Buick to restore. Even more important, I wish I could have one more chance to open that car door and sit up tall and proud beside my dad. But that was beyond what I could do as a 13-year-old. I was too embarrassed to know who I truly was. It would take a few more years, and a lot more experience, to own my A.C.T.

—

YOUR A.C.T.: GROUNDED IN HUMILITY, SELF-AWARENESS

Knowing your A.C.T. starts with humility. If we're not humble, we'll never be self-aware, and without self-awareness, we'll never learn and grow.

Self-awareness encompasses your strengths and blind spots, your skills and experiences, what you're passionate about, your sense of purpose, what motivates you.

One of our firm's early thought leaders, the late David McClelland, published seminal books that addressed motivation: *The Achieving Society* (1961), *Human Motivation* (1973), and several others. In his breakthrough work, McClelland identified three motivators that have the biggest effect on behavior in the workplace:

- **ACHIEVEMENT**
  defined as the desire for mastery
  at the individual level

- **AFFILIATION**
  meaning to establish and
  maintain relationships

- **POWER**
  in this context having an
  impact or influence

Which of these three describes you? Does the desire for achievement (mastery) get you out of bed each morning? Is it affiliation (relationships and belonging to a group)? Or is it the desire for power (influence)?

Ask yourself: *What energizes me? What's my motivation?*

Don't say money. Research shows time and again that it really isn't most important. Of course, compensation matters, and it must be fair. However, there is much more to consider than just your current title and salary. Your motivations—or drivers—are part of what makes you, you! By taking an honest look at yourself—your traits, competencies, drivers, and experiences—you will see who you are. Not only that, but you'll also gain insights into what you need to develop so you can transform yourself into who you want to become.

—

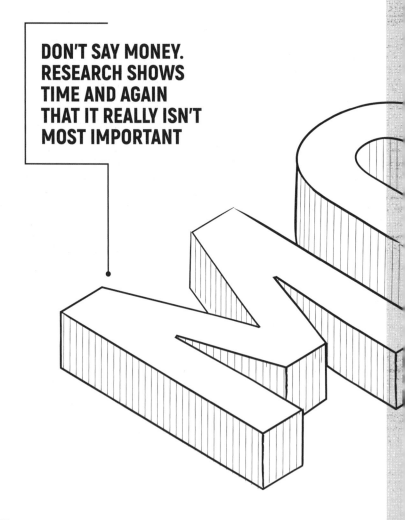

DON'T SAY MONEY. RESEARCH SHOWS TIME AND AGAIN THAT IT REALLY ISN'T MOST IMPORTANT

A LOOK IN THE MIRROR

To "know thyself," you need to look in the mirror. It starts with self-reflection, giving yourself the time and space to ask yourself the important questions that define "who you are" and "what you do."

But don't stop there. As humans, we're social creatures—we learn more about ourselves in our interactions with others. Take the next step of reaching out to close friends, confidantes, mentors, and partners. Asking others how they see you is also good practice for soliciting and embracing feedback.

ASKING OTHERS HOW THEY SEE YOU IS ALSO GOOD PRACTICE FOR SOLICITING AND EMBRACING FEEDBACK

WHO YOU ARE

TRAITS

These are the hardwired parts of your makeup.
For example:

- Are you more assertive or passive?
- Do you embrace or avoid risk-taking?
- How confident are you in what you
  know and what you can do?

DRIVERS

This is what motivates you. Your drivers can tell you
what kind of company culture and environment suit
you—even the type of boss you should work for.
For example, which of these are you motivated by?

- **Challenge:** Overcoming obstacles and
  taking on tough assignments

- **Power:** Achieving work-related status
  and influence, with greater visibility in the
  organization

- **Independence:** Taking an entrepreneurial
  approach, with greater freedom from
  organizational constraints to pursue your
  own vision

- **Collaboration:** Working interdependently
  in a group to pursue goals and achieve work-
  related success

WHAT YOU DO

COMPETENCIES

These are the skills and abilities you possess.
For example:

- In today's environment, it's not just about managing ambiguity—it's ambiguity on steroids. Amid an unprecedented amount of uncertainty, can you handle an ever-increasing level of ambiguity? How do you find a way forward when the way is unclear?

- What have you learned about yourself over the past few years? What skills and abilities have you developed that, perhaps, you never knew you had? How have you adapted to the new workscape—whether virtual, hybrid, in-person, or even on the front lines? How will you use this knowledge about yourself and your competencies going forward? How will that make a difference in your career—and how you impact others?

- Are you a lifelong learner who is insatiably curious—not just about your world, but also about the broader world? Do you look at new situations and challenges with a wide-angle lens, encompassing as much as possible?

- Are you open to diversity in all its forms—gender, race, and ethnicity—as well as backgrounds, perspectives, and ideas? Do you truly view inclusion as a source of greater creativity and innovation—and, if so, how?

- What is your purpose? This is the sense of personal mission and vision that gets you up in the morning. Even if you're in the early stages of your career and still discovering your purpose, there are probably things that ignite your passion.

FINDING YOUR PURPOSE

*When I am at my best—when I feel like
I am running on all cylinders—what am
I doing in that moment?
How does that make me feel?
The answer will help point you toward
your purpose.*

EXPERIENCE
This encompasses your story and your accomplishments. Consider:

- Events that have changed your life
- Failures you have faced, both personally and professionally, and the lessons learned from them

THE SIX STAGES OF CAREER DEVELOPMENT

With greater self-awareness, you can more deeply engage in your career journey. Although it is different for everyone, there is a master plan that governs just about any journey, as defined by the Six Stages of Career Development.

These Six Stages can help you calibrate where you are and where you're headed.

• THE FIRST STAGE: FOLLOWER

At phase one, you are a follower. Typically, this is associated with a first professional job out of college. As a follower, you are action-oriented and task-focused as you carry out what others tell you to do. After all, you will never lead if you don't know how to follow.

• THE SECOND STAGE: COLLABORATOR

You're still operating from your technical skill set, but you begin to develop people skills through collaboration.

· THE THIRD STAGE: INSTRUCTOR

As a first-time team leader or manager, you're tapping your people skills when you give instructions to your team, which may comprise only one person. The key here is whether you effectively instruct people on what needs to be done, instead of being the one to do it. Jobs that help you progress at this level include:

- *Staff Leadership* At this level, you have the responsibility but not the authority. Typical examples include planning projects, installing new systems, troubleshooting problems, and negotiating with outside parties.

- *Staff to Line Shifts* This involves moving to a job with an easily determined bottom line or result, managing bigger scope or scale, and taking on unfamiliar assignments.

· THE FOURTH STAGE: MANAGER

You are overseeing others by giving them objectives, as well as the means to pursue and achieve them. You may be managing people whom you've never met (or interviewed) in person— and who have never met each other face to face. And you're not just managing people, you're also managing change.

· THE FIFTH STAGE: INFLUENCER

At this stage, you transition away from directly managing a team to influencing people, especially those who do not directly report to you. Influence is a key leadership skill that you need to develop in order to work with people across the organization, especially those who do not report to you. In fact, you could be influencing people who are at your level or even more senior.

> **INFLUENCE IS A KEY LEADERSHIP SKILL THAT YOU NEED TO DEVELOP IN ORDER TO WORK WITH PEOPLE ACROSS THE ORGANIZATION**

· THE SIXTH STAGE: LEADER

At this level, you spend much of your time empowering and inspiring others. As a leader, you don't tell people what to do; rather, you engage them on what to think about. Within that context, your biggest priority is elevating people so that they can achieve more. This is absolutely grounded in your A.C.T.—being authentic, vulnerable, empathetic, and letting your humanness show to connect genuinely with others.

—

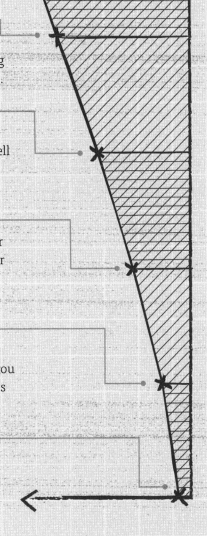

LEADER

At this level, you spend much of your time empowering and inspiring others.

INFLUENCER

At this stage, you transition away from directly managing a team to influencing people.

MANAGER

You are overseeing others by giving them objectives, as well as the means to pursue and achieve them.

INSTRUCTOR

As a first-time team leader or manager, you're tapping your people skills when you give instructions to your team.

COLLABORATOR

You're still operating from your technical skill set, but you begin to develop people skills through collaboration.

FOLLOWER

At phase one, you are a follower.

AN ENDURING A.C.T. IN
AN UNCERTAIN WORLD

One thing is certain: Today doesn't look like yesterday—and tomorrow won't look like today. We're in the midst of cataclysmic change in the workscape, the likes of which we haven't seen since the Industrial Revolution. To survive, you need to be relatable—and relevant. People need to know who you are and what you have to offer.

Now and in the future, that's the essence of the story you have to tell—your A.C.T. that defines you.

—

WE'RE IN THE MIDST OF CATACLYSMIC CHANGE IN THE WORKSCAPE, THE LIKES OF WHICH WE HAVEN'T SEEN SINCE THE INDUSTRIAL REVOLUTION

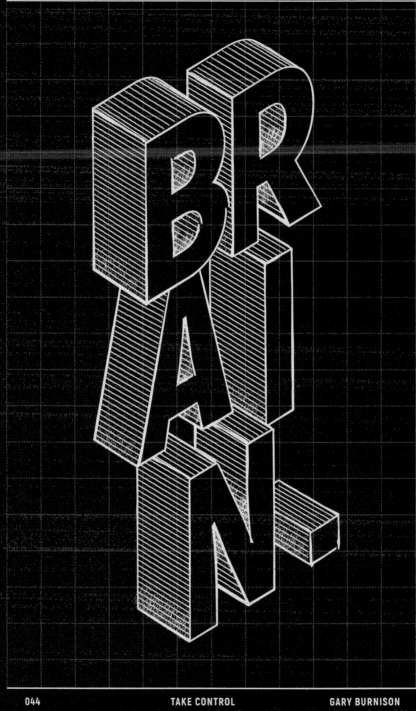

TAKE CONTROL **GARY BURNISON**

Chapter 2
TAPPING YOUR RIGHT BRAIN

M ost of us have lived in a largely left-brain world—overly focused on our technical skills. But the "future of work" that everyone is talking about is not about just our left brains. We need another skill set—to get context, make connections, and collaborate with others.

It's not that the left brain doesn't matter. But to take control and advance in your career, you need to tap your right brain—and that's all about forging relationships and inspiring, influencing, and motivating others.

—

KNOW YOUR BRAIN

LEFT-BRAINED

Logical, analytical, and objective. Practical and pragmatic. Detail- and fact-oriented. Prefer to think in words and numbers.

RIGHT-BRAINED

Relationship-builder. Connect and collaborate easily with others. Intuitive, creative, and free thinking. Tend to think in terms of visuals.

A TALE OF
TWO BRAINS

Let's put this in perspective. Early in your career, you were hired for your left-brain skills, which made you a good individual contributor—someone who would get the job done. But once you reach a certain level, it's a given that you possess left-brain skills— they're the table stakes.

The higher up you go, the more the right brain rules! Right-brain skills are anchored in what's called "social

BECOMING A RIGHT BRAIN THINKER

If you're naturally left-brained, you can develop right-brain capabilities. Here are a few suggestions:

• BE OPEN TO NEW IDEAS AND APPROACHES

Instead of defaulting to the tried-and-true (which appeals to your pragmatic side) be open to varied approaches and new ideas.

• EMBRACE AMBIGUITY

Practice coping with uncertainty and making decisions without having all the information beforehand.

• TEST YOUR SOCIAL LEADERSHIP SKILLS

Motivate, influence, and connect more deeply with others. You might find you enjoy it—and even that you're good at it!

leadership"—influencing, motivating, and inspiring others.

I discovered this early in my career. With an accounting background, I went to work right out of college for what is now KPMG and spent many years in consulting. As I interacted with clients and colleagues, I quickly saw that while my left-brain skills in finance and accounting were a great foundation, I needed to hone my people skills. Years later, when I joined Korn Ferry and became an operating officer and then CFO, I still needed my left-brain skills, such as thinking strategically and managing risk. Then I became CEO, and I needed to draw on my right brain more than ever to motivate, inspire, be highly attuned, and display optimism in the face of challenges.

As you take control, you'll find yourself moving beyond your left brain alone. At every phase and stage of your career, look for jobs and assignments that develop a full slate of skills—drawing on your left and right brains.

—

IT STARTS WITH SELF-AWARENESS

So how do you know what you need to become more right-brained? Like any skill development, you need to see yourself accurately.

NOT EITHER/OR–
IT'S BOTH!

These days, paradoxes abound—perform vs. transform, speed vs. significance, critique vs. create, execute vs. engage, head vs. heart. And one that I've seen a lot of lately is self vs. system—which can be expressed simply as "I vs. we."

We might be tempted to view left brain vs. right brain in the same way—another compare-and-contrast exercise like we did when we were in school.

Dogs vs. cats. Astronomy vs. astrology. Apples vs. pears. Spider-Man vs. Captain America. It was 11th grade English class, and as soon as the teacher began writing an endless list of topics on the blackboard, I knew what was coming.

The dreaded compare-and-contrast essay.

Panicked (the clock was ticking), I'd divide a piece of paper in half and start writing as fast as I could. Similarities on one side and differences on the other. Astronomy and astrology are both about planets—or is one about stars? Spider-Man and Captain America—wait, aren't they both Avengers? After a while, I had so many cross-outs and arrows, the only thing I could be sure of was my name at the top of the paper.

With all due respect to what we learned in 11th grade, the world today is not one or the other—or one versus another. The good news is we don't have to choose between the opposites. We can find the connections and congruencies between them.

> THE GOOD NEWS IS WE DON'T HAVE TO CHOOSE BETWEEN THE OPPOSITES. WE CAN FIND THE CONNECTIONS AND CONGRUENCIES BETWEEN THEM

And when it comes to how we interact and experience the world, it's not left brain or right brain. To be well-rounded people, we need both brains to bring the best of ourselves and our capabilities to everything we do.

The challenge, however, is that most people rely too much on their left brains—the technical skills and competencies that have gotten them this far. The truth is that even if you have deep and valuable expertise in a particular area—a real left-brain specialization—you still need people skills to collaborate with others.

It's a simple fact of life: What got us here, won't get us there. To get out of the left-brain trap, we need to tap our right brains.

Often, the difference between advancing or getting stuck comes down to self-awareness. In our research, we've found that, all things being equal, self-awareness usually explains why some leaders succeed and others fail. Raising your self-awareness can keep you from derailing.

Self-awareness is also at the heart of emotional intelligence (EI) and influences your ability to develop other competencies. A common problem among people who aren't self-aware is they overestimate their strengths and underestimate their weaknesses. As we discussed in Chapter 1, you need accurate self-knowledge to clearly see your strengths and weaknesses, abilities and competencies, and passion and purpose, as well as the drivers that motivate you.

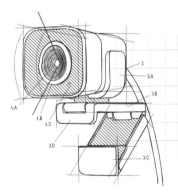

ENGAGE IN SELF-REFLECTION BY ASKING YOURSELF PROBING QUESTIONS: WHAT OLD BEHAVIORS ARE HOLDING YOU BACK?

Engage in self-reflection by asking yourself probing questions: What old behaviors are holding you back? Where do you feel you need to improve? What do you do well and with confidence? Are you relying too much on your left-brain technical skills? Do you really possess the right-brain capabilities to influence and inspire others?

And don't just take your own word for it—seek out informal feedback from others. What does your boss say about your work performance? What feedback are you getting from your mentor and coach? By combining feedback from others with the fruits of your self-reflection, you'll deepen your self-awareness.

But it doesn't stop there. Daniel Goleman, who is an expert in emotional intelligence, takes self-awareness a step further—adding emotion into the mix for emotional self-awareness.

When you're emotionally self-aware, you understand your own emotions and their effects on your performance. As Goleman explains, "You know what you are feeling and why—and how it helps or hurts what you are trying to do. You sense how others see you and so align your self-image with a larger reality. You have an accurate sense of your strengths and limitations, which gives you a realistic self-confidence."

Emotional self-awareness isn't something that you achieve once and then you're done with it. Rather, you are constantly presented with opportunities to be self-aware, and in each moment you must choose. By drawing on your emotional intelligence and your self-awareness every time you can, you will make it an ingrained habit. You will be known for being emotionally self-aware— with strong right-brain capabilities.

—

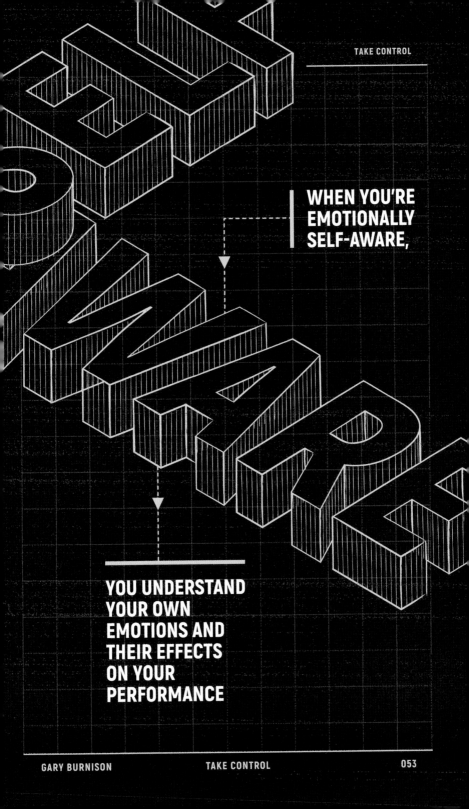

WHEN YOU'RE EMOTIONALLY SELF-AWARE,

YOU UNDERSTAND YOUR OWN EMOTIONS AND THEIR EFFECTS ON YOUR PERFORMANCE

DEVELOPING EI AND YOUR RIGHT BRAIN

Building your right brain is a discipline like any other—you need new habits, practice, and feedback. Here are some ways you can develop and exercise your EI and other right-brain skills.

• EMOTIONAL SELF-AWARENESS

Pay attention to situations that cause a physical reaction—a blush when you're embarrassed, your heart racing when you're excited or frightened, or sweaty palms when you're nervous or stressed. Become aware of what triggers these reactions and why. Notice the links between the physical signs, how you react to them, and the feelings that result. Consider keeping a log of your feelings and physical responses to help you become more emotionally self-aware.

• EMOTIONAL SELF-CONTROL

Develop strategies to help you stay in control and keep your cool in difficult situations. A few simple steps can make a difference—counting to 10 really does help! Or step outside for a breath of fresh air, change rooms, get water. Think the opposite of the emotion that's being triggered; if you're feeling angry, think of something funny or silly, or sing a song in your head. It works! Years ago, the catcher on my son's baseball team suddenly couldn't throw the ball back to the pitcher. He was a great player, so it wasn't an issue of skill or physical ability. With lots of fans in the stands, he just couldn't make the simplest of throws. Balls bounced off the pitcher's mound—a few times the ball skyrocketed to the outfield. The catcher was thoroughly disappointed and embarrassed. Opposing players would mock him. It was a nightmare. Then one day, as I sat in the stands behind home plate, I heard someone singing "Mary Had a Little Lamb." Then I noticed the catcher was making every throw without a single error. I later learned that the catcher had been advised by a former professional catcher to stop obsessing over every throw by singing a nursery rhyme to himself. We, too, will have days when we need to elevate our myopic focus to a broader horizon with a mantra, a purpose, visualization, or perhaps even our own version of "Mary Had a Little Lamb"—whatever it takes to contextualize. These kinds of pauses can help us gain perspective—and maybe even keep us from making a rash response.

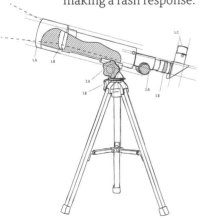

WE, TOO, WILL HAVE DAYS WHEN WE NEED TO ELEVATE OUR MYOPIC FOCUS TO A BROADER HORIZON

• A POSITIVE OUTLOOK

See the good in others and in situations. Challenges are viewed as opportunities to grow, learn, do things differently, and achieve better outcomes. That doesn't mean you won't feel stressed or worried at times, but a positive outlook can help you navigate those feelings and stay positive. For example, when you feel worried, afraid, or anxious, ask yourself: "What's really the worst thing that could happen? How could I deal with that?" Then consider, "What's the best that could happen? What if all goes well?" Focus on what the outcome will look like and feel like. Then channel your energy and enthusiasm toward making things go the way you want.

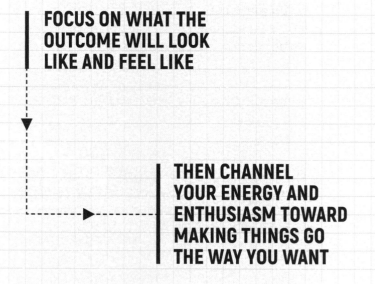

FOCUS ON WHAT THE OUTCOME WILL LOOK LIKE AND FEEL LIKE

THEN CHANNEL YOUR ENERGY AND ENTHUSIASM TOWARD MAKING THINGS GO THE WAY YOU WANT

- ## EMPATHY

To understand others is to truly hear and understand their thoughts, feelings, and concerns, whether spoken or unspoken. Ask yourself these questions to help gauge your level of empathy and see how you can improve in this EI competency.

- **When you listen,** do you truly pay attention to what the other person is saying? Or, do you lose focus? Are you thinking about what you can say next?

- **Do you pay** attention to cues that are verbal (tone of voice, speed, loudness, word choice) and nonverbal (hand gestures, facial expression, posture, eye gaze) to understand what's really being said?

- **Do you make** assumptions?

- **Do you ask** questions to better understand what the person is saying, feeling, or needing?

- **Do you provide** feedback—verbal and nonverbal—so that others know you are listening and interested?

By developing these skills and behaviors, you'll improve your ability to manage yourself and interact with others. As a result, you'll distinguish yourself as someone with a well-developed right brain.

—

RIGHT-BRAIN EMOTIONAL SKILLS

EMPATHY

Having concern for and awareness of others' feelings, problems, and motivations.

ASSERTIVENESS

Enjoying taking charge and directing others; being decisive.

INFLUENCE

Motivating and persuading others; being adept at interpersonal relationships.

SOCIABILITY

Enjoying interactions with others; being energized by the presence of others and easily initiating social interactions.

WHAT GREAT LOOKS LIKE

I f you wanted to be a great golfer, you'd probably study how a PGA Tour champion swings—or for basketball, one of the all-time NBA greats. If tennis is your passion, you'd watch every Wimbledon match. Even in our wildest dreams, of course, few of us are likely to attain that level of greatness (no matter how much we might wish). But who else would you want to emulate?

We take the same approach when it comes to career advancement. Our researchers have spent years figuring out the skills and traits that have gotten people ahead. Drawing from assessments of nearly 30,000 people at the entry level, mid-level, and C level, at Korn Ferry we compiled high-performance profiles that define what it takes to be great at each of these levels. Here, we'll look at how greatness is defined in two areas: First, how great leaders handle novel and uncertain situations (Figure 1). And second, how great leaders relate to or interact with others (Figure 2).

Starting with Figure 1, we can see how the following key traits (most of them right-brain capabilities) relate to performance in the context of handling novel and uncertain situations.

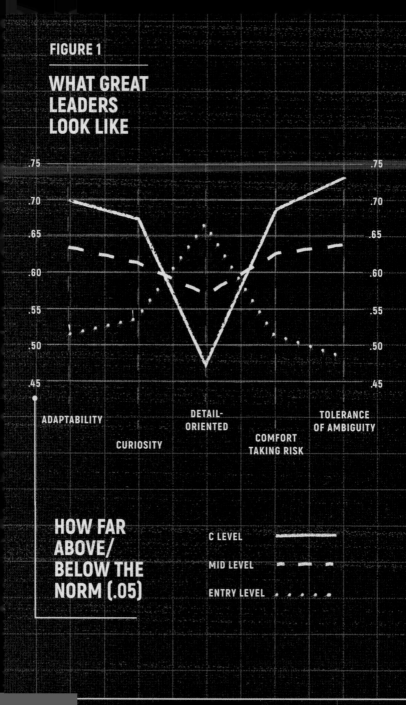

FIGURE 1

WHAT GREAT
LEADERS
LOOK LIKE

ADAPTABILITY

CURIOSITY

DETAIL-
ORIENTED

COMFORT
TAKING RISK

TOLERANCE
OF AMBIGUITY

HOW FAR
ABOVE/
BELOW THE
NORM (.05)

C LEVEL

MID LEVEL

ENTRY LEVEL

GARY BURNISON

Focusing on the middle of the graph, we can see that being detail-oriented is a trait that makes an entry-level person great (remember, it's a left-brain skill). Here, the expectation is that employees will carry out their assigned tasks and responsibilities as instructed. The greater the focus on detail at the entry level, the more coworkers and bosses can count on assignments being completed thoroughly and accurately. In fact, detail orientation is so important, it is the peak for the high-performing entry-level employee.

For the middle manager and especially for the C-level leader, detail orientation appears less pronounced (a lower target to hit), but it remains an important aspect of being an effective leader. These executives are still concerned with the details, knowing that they can make or break any plan or strategy. However, at the mid-level and especially at the C level, high performance means successfully delegating to others. At mid-level or as a senior leader, getting personally bogged down in the details is actually ineffective and could lead to not having the necessary mental bandwidth to focus on strategy.

From entry level to mid-level, we see that excellence means ramping up in adaptability and tolerance of ambiguity, both of which come with experience, particularly involving decision-making and taking on greater responsibility. These two traits are developed even further at the C level, where high-performing leaders must be extremely adaptable and highly tolerant of ambiguity, so they not only react to change but also initiate it.

Finally, at all three levels, curiosity is a distinguishing trait. For the high-performing entry-level person, curiosity goes beyond the normal learning curve and includes taking the initiative to soak up new experiences and build new skills. For mid-level managers who distinguish themselves, curiosity leads to competencies in new areas, such as taking on stretch assignments that are almost beyond their capabilities, or immersing themselves in the unfamiliar, such as working in a different country or region. For the C-level leader, curiosity prompts engagement in lifelong learning, which is a prerequisite to greatness.

CURIOSITY LEADS TO COMPETENCIES IN NEW AREAS, SUCH AS TAKING ON STRETCH ASSIGNMENTS OR IMMERSING OURSELVES IN THE UNFAMILIAR

Now, in Figure 2, we move to the emotional qualities that define high performance in how people interact with others. As the graph shows, the entry-level person is the mirror opposite of the mid-level manager and the C-level executive in both assertiveness and influence. While some people are naturally more assertive than others, it is a quality that can be developed with time and experience. For example, you can take on assignments to lead projects and, eventually, to lead people.

ADAPTABILITY

Being comfortable with unanticipated changes
and diverse situations; able to adjust to
constraints and rebound from adversity.

CURIOSITY

Approaching problems in novel ways; seeing
patterns and understanding how to synthesize
complex information; having the desire to
achieve deep understanding.

COMFORT TAKING RISKS

Ability to take on and handle risk. (Higher-level
positions typically involve more high-risk and
high-profile situations.)

TOLERANCE OF AMBIGUITY

Being comfortable with uncertainty and willing
to make decisions and plans in the face of
incomplete information.

Influence, not surprisingly, is a low point for the inexperienced entry-level person, but far more developed for the high-performing middle manager—and a key strength for great leaders. Highly adept C-level leaders leverage their influence and their network to align the team behind unifying goals and a sense of mission.

THE TWO ENDS OF THE EMOTIONAL SPECTRUM AS DEPICTED HERE—EMPATHY AND SOCIABILITY—SHOW COMPARATIVELY LITTLE DIFFERENCE AT ALL LEVELS

The two ends of the emotional spectrum as depicted here—empathy and sociability—show comparatively little difference at all levels. The high-performing entry-level person who must rely on others for coaching and mentoring is very focused on the needs of others—more so than mid-level and C-level leaders. Sociability is nearly equal at the mid-level and C level, given the need for these high-performing leaders to interact easily with others. But entry-level people who distinguish themselves are not far behind, displaying people skills that ingratiate them with others and enable them to interact with peers and with colleagues in positions several levels above their own.

—

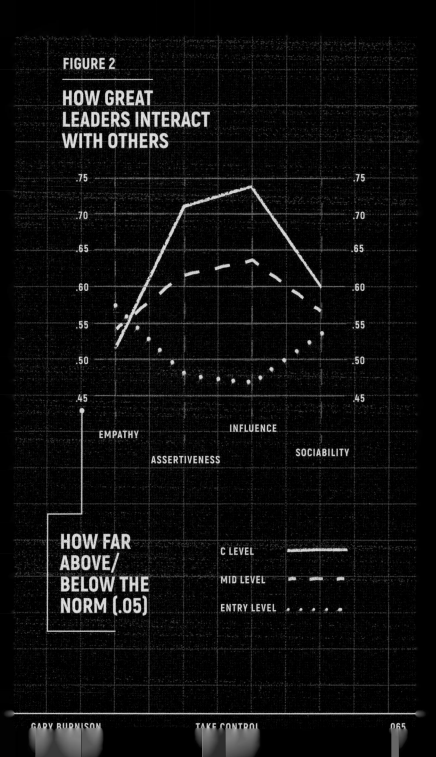

FIGURE 2

HOW GREAT LEADERS INTERACT WITH OTHERS

EMPATHY

ASSERTIVENESS

INFLUENCE

SOCIABILITY

HOW FAR ABOVE/ BELOW THE NORM (.05)

C LEVEL

MID LEVEL

ENTRY LEVEL

WHERE INSPIRATION MEETS EXASPERATION

His assessment was off the charts. This candidate had checked all the boxes in almost every leadership trait and skill—except for one: self-awareness. On his assessment graph, that quality sunk like a stone. I was curious, but one minute into our conversation, I knew exactly why. I started with smalltalk, but he wasn't having it. He launched immediately into a long, one-sided conversation—a litany of everything he had done.

For 36 minutes (yes, I timed it) he talked—at me, not to me. He must have used "I," "me," and "my" 200 times—that's more than five "I's" per minute. My team, my company, I run ... Whoa! I thought to myself. What was he running—a herd of cattle? Seriously, what about everyone else?

As I listened, I couldn't ignore the nagging question in my head. As good as his left-brain technical skills were, without the right brain how could he ever inspire anyone? At the end of his filibuster, he was parched—and I was exasperated.

THE RIGHT-BRAIN HABIT

Just as you improve your health and wellness by adopting better nutrition and exercise habits—daily, weekly, and monthly routines—you need a similar approach for your right-brain skills development. The following are prompts for self-reflection on a daily, weekly, and monthly basis. Choose the questions that resonate with you—and change it up or add your own later.

—

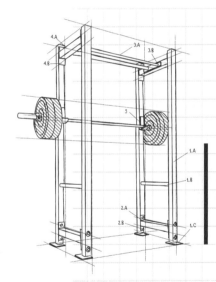

THE FOLLOWING ARE PROMPTS FOR SELF-REFLECTION ON A DAILY, WEEKLY, AND MONTHLY BASIS

YOUR DAILY DOSE

Each day, reflect on questions that can put your work life into perspective, while building the self-awareness, adaptability, and empathy that comprise right-brain skills.

- How have I contributed positivity or negativity to my team and others around me?

  ....

  ....

  ....

- What could I do differently to make someone feel better after an interaction they had with me versus how they felt before?

  ....

  ....

  ....

- How many times did I say thank you? ....

- How many times did I complain about something or someone? ....

- How did I maintain composure under stress?

....

....

- How many new people did I interact with and make a positive impression on today?

....

....

....

- Did I listen more—or talk more?

....

....

....

- What did I learn today?

....

....

....

....

YOUR WEEKLY WORKOUT

Just as you might devote one day a week to cross-training as part of your fitness routine, pick from the following list of questions to help exercise your right-brain skills.

- What situations could I have handled differently— not just through my words, but also my nonverbal cues (facial expressions, tone, and body language)?

....

....

....

....

- Which two people will I do something specific for this week?

1) ....

2) ....

- Whom can I ask for perspective about a challenge or problem I'm facing?

....

....

- Whom have I neglected to appreciate out loud?

  ....

  ....

- What efforts of others have I overlooked?

  ....

  ....

  ....

- Am I sharing more criticism or praise?

  ....

  ....

  ....

  ....

- Have I shared credit with others?

  ....

  ....

  ....

MONTHLY MILESTONES

Since habits develop over time, monthly check-ins will show how you're progressing.

- What motivated me the most this month and what will keep me motivated next month?

  ....

  ....

  ....

- What is the one achievement I can point to for the month?

  ....

  ....

  ....

- How am I "trending"—what feedback am I receiving?

  ....

  ....

  ....

- What new experiences did I try—a new activity, unfamiliar cuisine, different music style, etc.?

....

....

....

- How do my strengths meet the needs of the people around me?

....

....

....

- What examples from life, literature, sports, or entertainment inspire me or can help me through any challenges I'm facing?

....

....

- How am I celebrating others?

....

....

Over time and with practice, you'll become more self-reflective and self-aware. You'll understand your true strengths, have better clarity to identify and work on your weaknesses, and achieve a better balance between left brain and right brain.

Rather than get stuck in a rut—or rely only on our left-brain skills—we need to expand our thinking. In fact, the more open our minds become, the more we can develop and tap the capabilities that allow us to make a positive impact. We can become right-brain thinkers who focus on relating to and inspiring others.

—

THE MORE OPEN OUR MINDS BECOME, THE MORE WE CAN DEVELOP AND TAP THE CAPABILITIES THAT ALLOW US TO MAKE A POSITIVE IMPACT

TAKE CONTROL **GARY BURNISON**

Chapter 3

LEARNING IT ALL

I t's the secret to sustainable success: If you're happy, you're motivated, and if you're motivated, you're going to outperform. And a big driver of being happy and being motivated can be learning!

This may be surprising but think about it: Learning is the pathway to bigger and better opportunities, and that translates into greater engagement and having the satisfaction that you're making a difference.

There are extrinsic benefits, too. Learning is the most significant determinant of how much you'll earn over your career. That's why every job you take should come with ample learning opportunities, so that you're better positioned for the next move ... and the one after that.

It's no surprise that people who are curious and take risks are often the best learners. Until you tackle challenging job tasks where you must perform and face a real risk of failing, you will not develop significantly.

This is the essence of learning from experience.

—

THE DRIVING LESSON

At age 13, I wasn't really ready—and I couldn't get a learner's permit for another year. But my dad took me to the cemetery parking lot to practice a little. Dad's old car was a "three on the tree"—a three-speed transmission with the shifter on the steering column. I can still remember the H pattern: first gear, second gear, third gear, reverse, with neutral in between.

With his hand on mine, he guided me through shifting from one gear to the next. He also had to grab the steering wheel a couple of times—like when I rounded a corner a little too sharply, jumped a curb, and nearly clipped a tombstone. It was a hands-on, old-school teachable moment—one I never forgot.

The first time any of us did anything—riding a bike, solving a Rubik's Cube, or folding origami—more often than not, someone showed us, instead of us trying to do it all on our own. Through the power of observation, we learned as if through osmosis—adjusting our progress, in real time. Along the way, we learned what to do and also corrected bad habits and misunderstandings before they became ingrained and harder to undo.

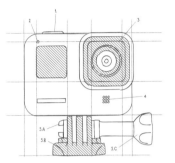

THE GOAL IS TO LEARN CONTINUOUSLY WITH A LIFETIME OF NEW CHALLENGES, DIRECT FEEDBACK, AND SELF-REFLECTION

And that set the pattern of learning for life.
The goal is to learn continuously with a lifetime of new challenges, direct feedback, and self-reflection.

—

THE 70-20-10

If you take nothing else from this chapter, here's the big message. Learning is life changing. Therefore, the main considerations for any job you take, more than your title or even your salary, are two key things: what you are learning and whom you are learning from.

The only way for any of us to get better is to surround ourselves with people who will challenge us. It's like in sports—when you're up against better players, you'll lose at first. But, in time, you'll up your game. In the workplace, seek to learn from and model the high performers—people who are better at what they do than you are.

This is where we meet the 70-20-10 rule of thumb for learning: 70 percent of your learning will happen on the job, including stretch assignments and challenging tasks; 20 percent will come from other people, especially your boss; and only 10 percent will come from formal training.

And that also means your boss has the most influence—accounting for 90 percent of your learning: providing access to those assignments and tasks (70 percent) and teaching you directly (20 percent). Ideally, your boss is often the best person to learn from. After all, who but your boss has the context of your current job responsibilities, your strengths and weaknesses, and how you need to stretch and grow to expand your contribution? So, when you choose the boss you'll be working for, choose wisely.

You'll also learn from coworkers, as well as mentors and coaches (whom we'll discuss in an upcoming chapter). But no matter whom you learn from, the best teacher is your experience.

—

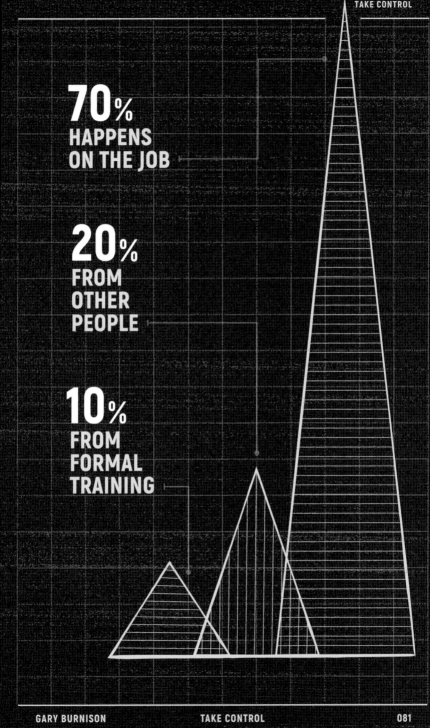

70% **HAPPENS ON THE JOB**

20% **FROM OTHER PEOPLE**

10% **FROM FORMAL TRAINING**

THE NO. 1 PREDICTOR OF SUCCESS

Lifelong learning is a process, and no one can say how that process will work for any one person. What we do know is we'll all have careers that evolve with changes in the world and the ongoing explosion of technology. It's up to us to keep pace by expanding our skills, competencies, and experiences.

Being adaptable means much more than swiping left and swiping right. It's all about what we've learned in the past and applying those lessons to new and first-time challenges and opportunities. This is learning agility— or what I call, "knowing what to do when you don't know what to do." Learning agility is so important, our firm considers it to be the No. 1 predictor of success.

The more learning agile you are, the better you can handle the complex and unexpected. So how do you know if you're learning agile? For one thing, you don't just deal with ambiguity—you actually embrace it. In addition, you tend to be reflective and insightful. You embrace new things and different approaches. And when things fail, you're willing to assume accountability and ultimate responsibility—while also looking for the lessons learned.

In short, you're constantly moving beyond the status quo and focusing on reinvention.

—

LEARNING AGILITY...
IN FOUR PARTS

SELF-AWARENESS

You are reflective, understand your strengths and blind spots, and seek feedback and personal insight.

MENTAL AGILITY

You embrace complexity, examine problems in unique ways, make fresh connections, and stay inquisitive. You're curious, with a wide range of interests.

PEOPLE AGILITY

You listen first and are open to diverse viewpoints. You challenge preconceived notions and use your emotional intelligence to refrain from making snap judgments about others.

CHANGE AGILITY

You're continuously exploring new options. You are good at devising what-if scenarios and can go from idea to implementation.

KNOWING
WHAT TO DO...

One of the best examples of learning agility—knowing what to do when the unexpected happens—occurred on a flight from Hawaii back to Los Angeles. We were already in our seats when the pilot boarded the plane. He wore a short-sleeve shirt, unbuttoned at the neck, and his hair was a little on the longer side. Strapped to his flight bags was a guitar.

"What are you going to play?" I asked him.

"Dylan," he replied with a smile.

"Oh, I love Dylan," I told him. A moment later I turned to my daughter; "This is going to be an interesting flight."

In the middle of this routine flight, with clear skies and no turbulence, our plane made an emergency evasive move—a sharp dive in a matter of seconds. Those gut-churning seconds felt like an hour on a runaway roller-coaster. When the plane stabilized, the fear was visible on the faces of passengers and flight attendants alike. Then came the eerie silence as we waited for what came next. Finally, the copilot made an announcement—something about another aircraft being in our airspace. That's when I knew we'd almost had a head-on collision.

Flash forward a week: While I was watching the news, a segment came on about a heroic pilot who averted what could have been the deadliest midair collision in history over the Pacific Ocean. That was our plane!

The hero was that laid-back, Dylan-playing pilot, who navigated in the moment because of his training, which had honed his skills to the point of becoming intuitive.

—

WHERE AMBIGUITY MEETS AGILITY

It's like we're all on an airplane these days—up in the air, and not sure of where or when we're going to land. When ambiguity is imposed on us, agility is our response. Combined, it's *ambigility*, and that's what will get us through.

The good news is we're not where we were. We've built new muscles, perhaps without even realizing it. We've become comfortable with being uncomfortable. When the world's ambiguity tests our agility, our response can be nothing short of ambigility. We're learning what to do when we don't know what to do amid circumstances and challenges we've never experienced before.

WHEN LEARNING STOPS

Complacency can be a killer. Often, it happens slowly—someone gets too comfortable in a position. Without enough challenges, learning stops, too.

This is what happened to someone I met through a mutual friend who reached out to me for advice. Unfortunately, this was after the fact when there wasn't much that I could do.

It all began when this person received a call from an in-house recruiter he knew, about a big job with room to grow but with only a modest salary increase from what he was currently making. He was interested, at least at first, but after thinking about it, decided he was comfortable where he was. The sticking point was that the job required more hours and more responsibilities. Not only that, but he'd be the new guy and would have to prove himself all over again.

FEAR OF FAILURE LED HIM TO INFLATE THE POTENTIAL RISKS THAT COME WITH TRYING AND LEARNING

Fear of failure led him to inflate the potential risks that come with trying and learning something new. Sadly, that fear made him turn down this promising job opportunity—and complacency set in.

LEARN IT OR
LEAVE IT

This is a great litmus test for judging whether you should stay in your current job or seek another opportunity:

· IS YOUR WORK MEANINGFUL?

Are you engaged in what you're doing? Does the organization you work for have a mission/vision/purpose that you can support and feel aligned with?

· WHOM ARE YOU WORKING FOR?

Are you working for a boss who champions you, who wants to help you grow and develop by giving you challenging assignments?

· ARE YOU LEARNING?

What new skills are you gaining?

Flash forward six months... Being comfortable in his job morphed into boredom. Every day felt the same, and regret nagged him as he thought back on that lost job opportunity. He reached out to the internal recruiter to say he was interested in pursuing something new, but instead received only a cool response.

—

IT'S NOT FAILURE...
IT'S CALLED LEARNING

The most important aspect of failure is not the moment of defeat or loss. Rather, it's what we do in the moment after that. It is never about failure—it is all about learning.

This attitude reframes failure as a combination of experience and experiment—failing and learning, re-experiencing and growing. After all, failure is usually temporary; it passes like a storm. So why would we let fear paralyze us? What are we really afraid of? Is it that we can't stand the possibility of failing?

The bigger question to ask ourselves is what greater accomplishment or goal could we strive for and achieve if we never gave into our fears? Across teams and organizations, what if learning from failure inspired courage?

Fail fast and learn faster. It turns adversity into agility, as we learn to see things in a new light and search for different answers and solutions.

—

OUR FIRST DAY OF CLASS

Ken Blanchard, the management expert with whom I've had some great discussions, often tells a story about his early days as a college professor. His habit was to give his students the answers to the final exam on the first day of class.

Because of this approach, he often found himself in trouble with other faculty members. Ken defended his decision by explaining his belief that his main job was to teach students the content they needed to learn—not to focus on evaluating them along some distribution curve. It's a concept he calls "Helping People Get an A," and Ken has applied it to work, as well.

Just as Ken found a different and sometimes unorthodox approach to teaching, we all need to be more open to new approaches around learning— especially in today's fast-changing environment.

We need to approach every new experience as the first day of class.

WHAT DO I NEED TO GET YOUR JOB ONE DAY?

WHERE POTENTIAL MEETS OPPORTUNITY

A few years ago, I was asked to be a guest lecturer at a university. The lecture hall was nearly full, and I looked out onto a sea of eager faces. Then, from the back row, a young man called out, "So, what do I need to get your job one day?"

"Clearly you all have potential or else you wouldn't be here," I told the students. "But how can you exceed that potential?"

The lecture hall was silent.

"It takes an abundance of opportunity," I suggested, and then the discussion went to another level.

We all sit at the intersection of potential and opportunity. Potential is the common denominator—we all have potential. But it will remain a mere fraction—substantially less than one—without the numerator of opportunity.

The challenge, though, is that potential is about tomorrow. Opportunity is about today.

Our progress is seldom linear. Life is full of setbacks: the time we got cut from the team. We didn't make the school band or get cast in the play. We didn't get the job we wanted—or the promotion went to someone else. In those moments, it can feel as if someone else controls our fate.

But who's to say what someone can or cannot do? Only with opportunity will we ever know. How do we give ourselves those opportunities? By always learning.

After all, knowledge is what we know. Wisdom is acknowledging what we don't know. Learning is the bridge between the two.

—

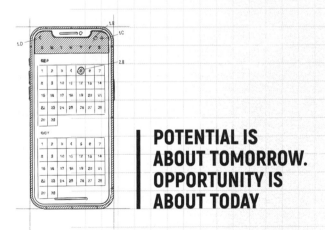

POTENTIAL IS
ABOUT TOMORROW.
OPPORTUNITY IS
ABOUT TODAY

HOW TO GET THE JOB – AND GET AHEAD

TARGETING

Chapter 4

NETWORKING AND TARGETING

One day, not long ago, I was sitting on a curb along a highway in Oklahoma. It was one of just a few trips I'd taken in almost a year and a half because of the pandemic, and I was driving a rental car along an unfamiliar road. Cell phone reception was sketchy, and I couldn't figure out which button in the car did what. So, with a conference call coming up, I pulled to the shoulder and found a place where the signal was strong, and my mind was clear.

That's when another vehicle pulled off the pavement and rolled to a stop a few feet from where I sat. A man and a woman got out, concern on their faces as they approached me. "Do you need help?" they asked. "Do you know where you're going?"

With sincere thanks, I assured them that I was fine. But in that moment, I also knew that, had I been lost or in need of assistance, they gladly would have helped me.

Looking back, I see that this brief encounter is also a metaphor for what we all need to progress in our careers—direction, input and feedback, and a helping hand to get us where we want to go.

Sometimes on the career journey, you'll be in the driver's seat, offering someone else a lift. Other times, you're the one on the side of the road, needing assistance. Everything in life goes in cycles—especially the labor market. A buyer's market turns into a seller's market and back again.

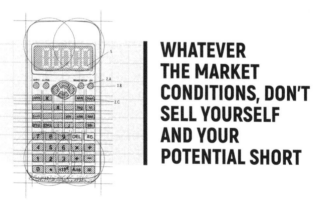

WHATEVER THE MARKET CONDITIONS, DON'T SELL YOURSELF AND YOUR POTENTIAL SHORT

Whatever the market conditions, don't sell yourself and your potential short. You need to understand the difference between the transaction of landing any job—and the process of identifying and getting the job you really want. And that's the goal of this chapter:

helping you find the position where you can be inspired and filled with purpose. In order to achieve, you need to thrive—and that means finding an environment in which you can flourish.

So what does that process look like? You need to do two things: First, targeting the right *opportunities* so you know where you'd like to go. Second, tapping your network so you can find people who can give you some advice and, ideally, make a warm introduction to a hiring manager.

If this sounds old school, it is. But it's more relevant than ever because we all need to reach out—intentionally, deliberately, and purposefully—to forge connections, and in different ways, with people we haven't seen in a while. It is a two-lane highway. In one direction, you are the one extending a helping hand to others as they try to get to their next career destination. In the other direction, you are the recipient of help and opportunities, including from mentors, sponsors, and coaches. Combined, this is targeting and networking at its best!

And here's what you'll probably find: Just like that couple in Oklahoma, most people you know will go out of their way for you. This is not a rescue—someone swooping in and plucking somebody else up, like a fish out of the ocean. Rather, it's all about engaging with others at all stages of your career, sometimes in unexpected places and interesting intersections.

—

THE FIRST STEP: TARGETING

No matter what the job market looks like—whether employers are scrambling to find people to fill positions or there are plenty of candidates for every job—the search for that next right opportunity starts the same way. You need to target.

You don't want just any job, whether within your existing employer or in another company. You want the right job where you will gain the skills and experiences you need to advance further. To find that kind of opportunity, you can't just be a seller, trying to convince an employer to hire you. You're also a discerning buyer, shopping for the right opportunity at an organization whose purpose you're aligned with.

This kind of thinking changes things, because it emphasizes how much choice you have in the matter. And that's why you want to target your next opportunity. Instead of looking everywhere and anywhere, you're zooming in on what makes the most sense for you—given who you are, what you can contribute, and the culture that best suits you. Most important, you are looking for that intersection where your purpose and the company's purpose align, in an environment where you can thrive.

—

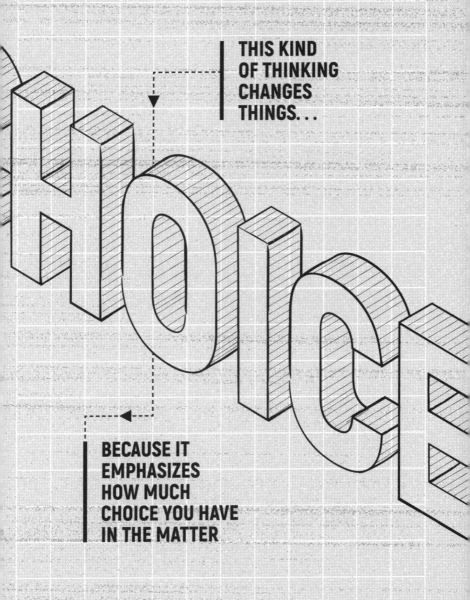

THIS KIND
OF THINKING
CHANGES
THINGS...

BECAUSE IT
EMPHASIZES
HOW MUCH
CHOICE YOU HAVE
IN THE MATTER

BACK TO
THE FUTURE

I ronically, we knew this intuitively when we were young. I was reminded of this not long ago when I took my kids to an ice cream shop. Sitting at a table in the corner was a teenager filling out a job application. Did that take me back to my high school days! In those days, you'd go to the place you wanted to work and ask if they were hiring. If the manager or owner wasn't busy, you'd get an "interview" on the spot. And if your friends worked there, they'd put in a good word for you. In fact, that's probably how you found out about the job in the first place, and a friend made a warm introduction to the manager for you.

But as our careers progressed, we often got the idea that we must wait for the job to come to us, or that we can be passive about our job search by just sending out resumes and hoping for the best. The process we understood so well as teenagers—and that worked so well in those early days—began to elude us. We forgot the fundamental rules that apply to all of us and at every level: You have to know where you want to go and then find someone who will open the door for you.

—

MAKING YOUR PLAN

To pursue your next opportunity, you need to have a plan. Think of it as a marketing strategy in which you are the product.

It starts by looking within—your skills and competencies. These are a significant part of what you bring to your next position, whether inside or outside your current workplace. What has made you successful thus far? For example, do you have a strong financial acumen? Are you naturally creative? Can you motivate others—and how have you done so in a virtual environment? How do you drive results by working with a team in multiple virtual locations, who may never see each other in person?

> **IT STARTS BY LOOKING WITHIN—YOUR SKILLS AND COMPETENCIES**

Once you understand more fully what you have to offer, now you can look at the opportunities you want to pursue—whether inside your current employer (perhaps another division or department) or with a new company.

Targeting covers three main points: location, companies and industries, and roles and responsibilities. Let's take a look at each.

01 LOCATION: WHERE YOU WANT TO LIVE AND WORK

A few years ago, this meant geography—the region, state, or city you wanted to live in or that you needed to stay in. If that meant California, you didn't look at jobs in New York. But that has been turned on its head. As remote working becomes institutionalized, more companies will likely downsize from their mega-office "mansions" to "cottages"—places to meet customers and accommodate in-person collaboration. Commuting probably won't be something that most people do every day; they'll do it occasionally.

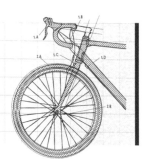

> **COMMUTING PROBABLY WON'T BE SOMETHING THAT MOST PEOPLE DO EVERY DAY; THEY'LL DO IT OCCASIONALLY**

All that adds up to more flexibility and the ability to target just about any company anywhere. But there's one caveat: You will probably need to get to a physical office at some point, particularly to develop relationships with others. Bottom line: As you consider location, think not only about where you want to live and work, but also the arrangements that would suit you—and your employer.

02 COMPANIES: WHERE YOU WOULD LIKE TO WORK AND WHY

You're making a wish list of the companies you admire—places where you could really see yourself working. Purpose is everything! When you truly feel aligned with the organizational purpose, you'll feel connected to something bigger than yourself—with the knowledge that what you do really does matter.

This is all about culture and fit. These days, defining culture is far more than just office space and real estate. (And there's a whole chapter on culture later on.) For now, suffice it to say that if you ask six people to define culture; you'll probably get 12 different answers. But it boils down to one thing: It's how work gets done. And that's all about the collective culture of the beliefs, behaviors, and shared mindset that influence actions and interactions.

As you think about the kind of company you'd like to work for, consider the type of environment in which you would thrive—for example, small, medium, or large firm. What environment suits you best—fast-paced, collaborative, casual, or corporate? How do people work together and interact? Can you deal with all-Zoom, all-the-time—or do you miss in-person interactions? Be honest with yourself! A lack of authenticity could lead you to pursue companies that would not be a good fit for you.

Getting feedback is an important part of the process. For example, reach out to someone you know, such as a former colleague who has joined your target company or a similar firm in that industry. Find out what it's like to work there. You're looking for the inside scoop on the culture and what it would be like to be an employee. Questions to ask include:

- What is it like to work there?

- Is it political? Bureaucratic? Entrepreneurial? Process-driven?

- Do employees get together to connect and collaborate?

- Does the company develop employees?

These questions will give you further insight into the company culture (e.g., traditional and hierarchical or flatter and more performance driven), as well as what your career path might look like there.

As you come up with your target companies, industries and sectors will obviously be an influence. For example, if you are a healthcare professional, you will most likely want to work for a healthcare company. But for many jobs—and especially in the dynamic technology industry—it's possible to move across sectors.

And speaking of technology, don't forget that virtually every company these days is in the technology business, from blue-chip industrial companies to tech startups. Your next best opportunity may emerge from a surprising place.

For more insight about your target companies, look on:

• SOCIAL MEDIA

Google the company name and see what comes up! Read news stories about the company. Check out their social media. Read the annual report. Listen to the latest earnings call recording. Obviously, the company's own website is also a good place to start, such as its mission and vision statements and the kinds of philanthropic activities it supports. Here are some things to consider:

- **The health of the company:** Is it growing or stagnant? What is the industry like?

- **The company's reputation:** You want to work for an employer that's known for its brands, its products/services, and the way it does business. Look at websites dedicated to company reputations. What are current and former employees saying? Has the employer been recognized on any lists as a best place to work? Is it known for its ESG commitment or corporate social responsibility?

- **The culture:** Talk to people who currently work at the company or were there recently. Does this sound like a place where you can do your best work, make an impact, and prove your value?

· LINKEDIN

Searching on LinkedIn for industries or sectors will give you a look at companies and the people who work at them. As you identify specific companies, you can also find out more about how they are regarded on their LinkedIn pages and blogs.

· GLASSDOOR

Read reviews of companies posted by current and former employees.

DOES THIS SOUND LIKE A PLACE WHERE YOU CAN DO YOUR BEST WORK, MAKE AN IMPACT, AND PROVE YOUR VALUE?

· SPECIALIZED SITES

These include Crunchbase for startups and Manta for small businesses.

· ALUMNI SITES AND GROUPS

Your college alma mater may offer career resources for alumni as well as graduating seniors. These can include networking events and opportunities (in-person or virtual) to hear speakers from various industries and companies.

· MOST ADMIRED LISTS

Magazines and organizations publish lists of "most admired" companies based on certain criteria that make them "best places to work" overall and in a variety of categories (for women, working parents, etc.).

· CHECK OUT THE PEOPLE LANDSCAPE

Are you connected (e.g., on LinkedIn) to any people at your target company? If so, how long have they been there? Where did these people come from—what are their qualifications? Do their profiles indicate that they've been promoted along the way? You won't get a complete org chart by any means, but you'll get a good view of the landscape within the company and about the specific role you're interest in.

03 ROLES AND RESPONSIBILITIES: THE JOB-SEARCH SPIRAL

This third phase of your targeting is like a spiral, with your current job in the center. If your job search is limited to opportunities based on your direct experience—for example, doing the same job for a similar company—you will not move too far out on the spiral. But you may go to a larger competitor or manage a larger team or bigger projects.

You may also look further out on the spiral, for example, in a neighboring industry sector—such as from pharmaceuticals to medical devices. With well-defined competencies, skills, and experiences that demonstrate what you can contribute, you'll probably be taken seriously by a hiring manager. This also applies when changing roles within the same sector—such as from marketing to sales.

Then there are the more dramatic changes, farther out on the spiral—a complete change in industry. Generally speaking, the more you move away from your center, the harder it will be to translate your skill set and industry knowledge. But it could provide the most personal growth.

—

SKILL SET

THE MORE YOU MOVE
AWAY FROM YOUR
CENTER, THE HARDER IT
WILL BE TO TRANSLATE
YOUR SKILL SET AND
INDUSTRY KNOWLEDGE

THE SECOND STEP: NETWORKING

The next step is finding someone who can help you get there. This is when it's important to have a strong network. But keep in mind the golden rule of networking—it's not about you.

Networking is about building relationships—and relationships aren't one-way streets. Ideally, networking is grounded in what you can do for others. It's the fruits of networking: When you need their help, the people you've helped in the past will be more likely to help you.

> ## IT'S THE FRUITS OF NETWORKING: WHEN YOU NEED THEIR HELP, THE PEOPLE YOU'VE HELPED IN THE PAST WILL BE MORE LIKELY TO HELP YOU

Be curious! Engage with everyone you meet. Find out who they are, where they work, what they are passionate about. Approach each conversation as an opportunity to learn more about people and the world. Above all, stay connected.

—

WHERE HONESTY MEETS AUTHENTICITY

To network with others, you need to let them see who you are—not merely show them some version of what you think they want to see.

I'll never forget the story. A person had the courage and candor to list "convicted felon" on her resume. She had been convicted of manslaughter after killing her horribly abusive spouse. She then called a hiring manager and asked, "Would you hire an ex-convict?"

After asking many questions and conducting extensive due diligence, the employer hired her. From what I hear, she's a great employee.

I'LL NEVER FORGET THE STORY

BUILDING YOUR REPUTATION

As you build and nurture your network, you're also building your reputation. People get to know not only your expertise, but, more importantly, your personality. All these factors come together when you need someone to vouch for you in a way that opens the door to your next job. Ideally, here's how this works:

There's an opening for a job you really want at the company that's the ideal fit for you. Your traits and competencies make you a great candidate for the position. Your experiences paint a picture of career progression that makes this job the logical next step. Instead of just sending out your resume, you search your network of contacts for someone to vouch for you. It may be someone you know directly, or you may have to network your way to get to "someone who knows someone."

Validation is not only good for you, it's also valuable to the company. Organizations today are trying to retain talent. While the reality of the career nomad isn't changing any time soon, getting people to stay four years instead of leaving after two (and turning those four years into eight) can be good for all involved. To reduce the risk of a bad fit or advancing someone too soon, companies want to know "the person," not just what they've done.

—

DON'T FORGET TO NETWORK WITHIN

Networking doesn't begin and end with getting your next job. You want to keep growing and nurturing your network—especially your network within the organization where you work. A lot of that used to happen organically—back when we had places to go and smalltalk used to happen in the hallways. Now, making those connections must be inorganic—we have to make it happen, deliberately and with intention.

The first step to building your network within is to lead with your give. What information, insight, or assistance can you offer? Have you heard someone mention they needed help with a project or initiative? Volunteer for an activity, whether that's in-person or virtual. It's a great way to lead with your "give."

Next, identify whom you want to meet and why. Instead of blasting out LinkedIn invitations, take a targeted approach. Know why you want to connect. Does someone who recently joined the firm have expertise in a different sector of the industry? Or does the person work in part of the firm that you don't know anything about and you're eager to learn more?

—

FINDING MENTORS, SPONSORS, AND COACHES

Somewhere in your growing network are probably three key people—someone to mentor you, someone to sponsor you, and someone to coach you (or to introduce you to a professional coach). They're not in the same role—so they're probably not the same person. Coaches speak to you; mentors speak with you; and sponsors speak for you.

—

MENTORS – TAKING OTHERS UNDER THEIR WINGS

The best situation would probably be to have mentors both inside and outside your company for multiple perspectives. A mentor outside your company might be a former boss. Those who are outside your workplace may particularly help with getting a broader view of your industry and position.

Ideally, your mentor is someone who has been on a similar career path to yours or who shares a similar vision of success. While you should have some similarities with your mentor, that doesn't mean you need to be (or should be) mirror images of each other. In fact, some of the most productive mentor-mentee relationships can be more like sparring partners than best friends. Having a mentor who is unlike you also helps you access diverse viewpoints. Lastly, your mentor is a sounding board and advisor, not a personal job coach. Your mentor can help you understand and navigate culture and politics and give some perspective from his or her own career journey.

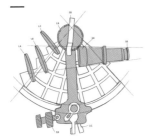

YOUR MENTOR CAN HELP YOU UNDERSTAND AND NAVIGATE CULTURE AND POLITICS

SPONSORS – ADVOCATING FOR OTHERS

A sponsor is likely to be someone higher up in the organization who can champion you. This is the person who can make the case for why you should get a particular assignment or promotion.

In contrast with a mentor who advises you, a sponsor advocates for you. One of my colleagues describes a sponsor as the person who mentions your name to others when you're not in the room. This is highly impactful—as research shows, people with sponsors are substantially more likely to move up in their careers than those without.

—

COACHES – FORMAL
AND INFORMAL

The role of a coach is to help you gain perspective and objectivity. Your coach is almost by definition someone outside the company. This is crucial because a coach brings an outsider's perspective with objectivity and knowledge, including what others in similar situations have done.

We know what coaching looks and feels like. We remember it well from the coaches and teachers—the ones who truly knew how to motivate and inspire—from elementary school playgrounds to classrooms and high school gymnasiums. Other than our parents, these were possibly the first people whose feedback really mattered to us—and whose influence shaped us for life.

In the same way today, a coach is also someone you can be vulnerable with, admitting your fears and anxieties or venting frustrations (another reason for this person to be outside the company). When that level of trust exists with a coach, you'll have the psychological safety to speak your mind—and bare your soul. For example, a coach can provide insight as to why you're unhappy in your current role or where you might be a better fit. Your coach's insights can help you create specific goals and develop a plan on how to achieve them.

—

A COACH'S WORDS
THAT LAST A LIFETIME

When I was 12, I went to a basketball camp led by Coach Gene Keady—a legend in Kansas. He went on to an acclaimed coaching career at Division 1 colleges, most notably Purdue where he was head coach for 25 years. Coach Keady was the first person to tell me I would be a leader one day.

Several months ago, I called Coach Keady, who is now in his 80s. It was the first time I'd spoken to him in decades. "Coach, you won't remember me, but you set the foundation that guided my life," I said. Coach Keady's response was simple: "That was exactly my purpose with the thousands of young people I had the privilege to coach—to change their life."

To this day, I remember the feeling I had, knowing these coaches believed in me, before I even believed in myself. That's what a coach does—and the impact of their words and actions lasts a lifetime.

TO THIS DAY, I REMEMBER THE FEELING I HAD

AN ONGOING PROCESS

My last word on targeting and networking is to remember that both are key elements of an ongoing process. You're always looking ahead for the next opportunity, and how you can access it—just as you are keeping an eye out for others and whom you might recommend for a position. You keep giving to your network: helping others, engaging with them via social media, and leading with your give. This will not only help keep your career on track, but you'll also be sharing your journey with others—and providing a helping hand along the way.

—

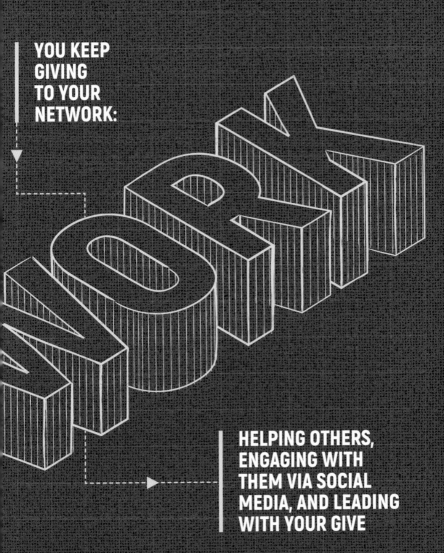

YOU KEEP GIVING TO YOUR NETWORK:

HELPING OTHERS, ENGAGING WITH THEM VIA SOCIAL MEDIA, AND LEADING WITH YOUR GIVE

Chapter 5

YOUR RESUME - THE NECESSARY EVIL

The resume has lost a lot of its weight over the years, especially to the LinkedIn profile and a positive, professional social media presence. And the fact is, recruiters and hiring managers spend only seconds on the initial screening of a resume. Once you make the cut, your resume will get a little longer look, but it's still usually less than five minutes.

That raises the question: Why bother with a resume? After all, the resume only accounts for about 10 percent of what it takes to get a new job—not the 90 percent that people assume.

The answer is simple. You still need one. But rather than something you either dash off quickly—or spend too many hours overwriting—a resume is best approached as part of your branding effort. It's not a standalone document, but rather part of a living document that includes your online presence. Together, this is how you describe your up-to-date skills and competencies, your accomplishments and experiences— with relevance for today's world.

THE FIRST "EYES" ON VIRTUALLY EVERY RESUME THESE DAYS IS A BOT

Keep in mind that the first "eyes" on virtually every resume these days is a bot. In fact, everything—your LinkedIn profile, career site postings, Facebook, and even that TikTok video—is fair game for bot crawlers that are identifying, evaluating, and categorizing you and your career.

Bots crawl all over publicly available information and through applicant tracking systems (ATS) used by 98 percent of the Fortune 500 to gather, analyze, and parse resumes and candidate profiles. Knowing this, your best defense against the bots is a good offense—and that's knowing how the game is played. If you're bot-savvy, you'll rise to the top. You may even find yourself becoming a passive candidate tapped for opportunities that match your background when you're not even looking for a job.

—

WHERE ARE THE PEOPLE?

I f you try to ignore the bots, though, you'll run the risk of having your resume disappear into a technology black hole. That's clearly what was happening to someone who came to me for advice on their frustrating job search. Despite having undergraduate and graduate degrees and an internship at a technology company, they weren't getting traction when applying for jobs online.

"What are they looking for?" they complained. "I'm a high achiever. I've got experience in a hot area. Why aren't these people seeing me?"

And that's the problem with their assumption. People weren't seeing their resume first—the bots were.

Most job seekers today read a posting online and tell themselves they're a perfect match. All they need to do is upload their resume and wait for a recruiter or hiring manager to call. But that contact never happens because the bots didn't flag their resume.

Even in a tight job market, the "spray and pray" approach is a losing proposition. Your only hope is to get the bots on your side.

—

ON CAREER WEBSITES AND COMPANIES' CAREERS PAGES, BOTS OFTEN ARE THE FIRST ENCOUNTERS

THE THREE BOTS
YOU'LL MEET

Across the job-search landscape,
bots fall into three basic categories:

01 THE CRAWLER BOT

These bots identify passive and active candidates by
scanning hundreds of millions of public profiles, as well
as applicants within a company's Applicant Tracking
System (ATS). For job seekers, it's a reminder to keep their
professional online presence up to date—and avoid those
hip-shot social media posts and flaming Tweets. Whether
you know it or not, you're being evaluated all the time.

02 THE CAREER
ASSISTANT BOT

On career websites and companies' careers pages, bots
often are the first encounters. Bots ask candidates about
their backgrounds and jobs they're seeking and offer
suggestions. Bots may even pose prescreening questions
to confirm eligibility. Candidates who pass are then
directed to another bot for an online assessment or a
video interview app to answer more questions. And it all
happens without any human intervention.

03 THE RECRUITER HELPER BOT

This bot works behind the scenes to help recruiters—sending reminders about candidates progressing through the screening and interviewing process, or who needs to be told they're no longer in the running. The objective is to cut recruitment time and improve the experience for candidates.

Understanding the bots, though, is only half the battle. The real trick is getting them on your side. You need to "SEO" yourself.

To get your resume validated by a bot, you need to mirror how websites use exact keywords to gain visibility with search engines. For example, if you're applying for a job that requires "good research capabilities," there's no need to search for the right wording to insert. Just say "good research capabilities." The closer your resume wording matches the job description, the better your chances. Avoid acronyms—if you're a certified PMP, spell out project management professional. Lastly, don't limit your descriptions to skills and experience—address culture fit, too. If you thrive in a fast-paced environment, can handle ambiguity, or lead collaborative and creative teams, then say so.

With that, let's go from the metaverse of the bots to the universal truths of writing a resume.

—

MARKETING YOURSELF

Ask five people how to write a great resume and you'll get 15 different answers. There are countless books and guides out there that focus only on how to write a resume. In this chapter, we're going to focus on the role of the resume, from the perspective of the company that places a professional in a new job every 3 minutes of the workday—and how to keep your online presence fresh and professional.

The purpose here is to talk about what your resume is supposed to do for you and how you can use it to help you tell your story.

Think of your resume as a marketing document for yourself that summarizes your experiences, shows that you match the qualifications of the job you're applying for, and gives a good indication of the quantifiable results you have achieved. Plus, your resume will also serve as a conversation guide for the interviews you'll be having, whether by phone, on screen, or in-person—or a combination of all three.

To do all that successfully, you'll need a resume that is concise yet thorough—a crucial balance to achieve.

—

YOU'LL NEED A RESUME THAT IS CONCISE YET THOROUGH

APPROACHING YOUR RESUME

FIVE RESUME TRUTHS

01. Don't lie. People will check your background. If one thing is doubtful, then everything can be doubted.

02. Don't inflate. Authentically represent your accomplishments.

03. Mind the time gaps. Don't try to smooth them over or fudge the dates; again, people will check.

04. Make it attractive to the eye. Include whitespace. Balance bold fonts for names, titles, and names of companies with regular fonts for descriptions. Use bullet points for accomplishments. Include action verbs.

05. Showcase your "brand." Your resume is a summary—an outline. You're conveying what you are known for—your brand— which must be continually defined and articulated as the story you tell.

Updating your resume or LinkedIn profile is time-consuming, so you may be tempted to put it off. Or you get paralyzed in the details—should you use Times New Roman or Calibri? Is can-do-attitude a noun or an adjective? And all of a sudden you think you are the Ernest Hemingway of resumes. There's no need to do this to yourself. The first new overhaul will involve some work, but as you update it regularly, the process will be far less painful going forward.

Here are some tips to writing and updating your resume:

• TAKE THE TV INTERVIEW APPROACH

In a TV interview, a person typically gets no more than 20 to 40 seconds to make a point. That's the goal here: Capture the most salient information about your recent accomplishments, quickly and concisely.

• DO SOME TIMED BRAINSTORMING

Give yourself a series of timed exercises that help you get to the most important material. Set a timer for two minutes and write five bullet points. These bullet points should include things about yourself, what you have done, a time when you overcame a challenge or exceeded your goals—particularly when pivoting to a remote-everything environment, your five biggest accomplishments, and your two biggest failures.

• UNDERSTAND THE PURPOSE

Your resume should concisely and compellingly illustrate one major message point: *This is how I made things better for my employer while I was there.*

THIS IS HOW I MADE THINGS BETTER FOR MY EMPLOYER WHILE I WAS THERE

• SEARCH AND DESTROY FOR MEANINGLESS PHRASES

As you review and revise your resume, scan for those meaningful words. Never describe yourself as "innovative," "energetic," "a team player," "a self-starter," or "a good communicator." These are so overused they have become meaningless.

• UPDATE YOUR RESUME AND LINKEDIN PROFILE

Using this script, update your resume and your LinkedIn profile. Proofread carefully by reading aloud. You don't want a typo to knock you out of consideration.

• CONTENT AND RELEVANCY MATTER MOST

A B+ resume (in terms of format and attractiveness) from someone with A+ experience will win over the inverse: a beautifully written A+ resume from someone with only B+ experience.

• NO GIMMICKS, PLEASE

Creative resume formats rarely help. In 95 percent of careers, gimmicks will only be a distraction. The only exception is if you are pursuing an artistic occupation to be, say, an art director, stage manager, or graphic designer. But even then, content matters.

GIMMICKS WILL ONLY BE A DISTRACTION

• TEST DRIVE YOUR RESUME

Reach out to a mentor or trusted advisor. Don't rely on a friend, spouse/partner, or family member—it's hard to get unbiased feedback from them, and criticism can make the relationship awkward. Ask someone who knows you professionally, whose opinion you value, whether your resume reflects who you are and what you bring to an organization.

• AVOID SHOTGUNNING

Resist sending your resume out blindly to everyone and anyone. Your resume is best viewed as a calling card after you've targeted and networked your way to a warm introduction.

• UPDATE IN REAL TIME

In an ideal world, you'll never have to pull your resume out of the mothballs. Instead, continually review, revise, and refresh this document—along with your online profile—on an ongoing basis, whether or not you're in the job market.

—

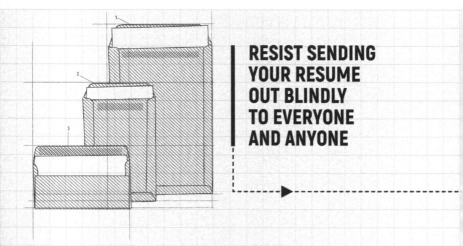

RESIST SENDING YOUR RESUME OUT BLINDLY TO EVERYONE AND ANYONE

KEY COMPONENTS
OF YOUR RESUME

With this understanding, we're going to walk through constructing parts of your resume. (Sample resumes can be found in the Appendix of this book.) Keep in mind that the content of your resume will depend on the stage of your career. For someone at the professional level, technical skills still matter and will be highlighted. A resume for someone at the director or manager level (or equivalent) is likely to be longer and more detailed in terms of technical skills than for someone at the C level, where what matters most is title, company, and accomplishments. And, of course, a professional-level resume contains more information than an entry-level resume.

—

PROFESSIONAL
SUMMARY

For someone whose technical skills speak volumes about their competencies and relate directly to their accomplishments, a professional summary at the top of the resume is an excellent way to convey information quickly and concisely.

For the hiring manager who is glancing at this resume immediately before and sometimes during the interview, the professional summary emphasizes meaningful skills and competencies.

PROFESSIONAL SUMMARY

Financial executive with extensive experience building and leading teams. Areas of expertise include:

- Strategic planning
- Business process reengineering
- Budget & cost management
- SEC reporting & governance
- Merger & acquisition integration
- Financial planning & analysis

Who needs a summary? Mid-level professionals with several years of experience, valuable technical skills, and expertise that relates directly to the contribution they will make to their next employer.

Who doesn't need a summary? Entry-level employees, including recent college graduates and those with only a few years of experience. In most cases, a professional summary would require stretching or inflating what they know or what they've done. It's most important to showcase the experience gained thus far—even if it's only one or two jobs.

C-level executives also don't need a summary because, for them, technical skills are assumed—the "table stakes" of their current and next position. C-level executives need to showcase four important aspects of their careers: the size of the companies they've led, the size of the teams they've led, a pattern of ever-increasing responsibilities, and what they've accomplished

—

SKIP THE OBJECTIVE

While many people believe their resume must have an objective, the problem is that they are usually either "too hot or too cold"— never "just right." They may be too broad or too specific. They can take away from the focus on what benefits you bring or make you seem pigeonholed. To say you're seeking a "challenging team leadership position" might be true, but it says nothing about what you can do for a prospective employer.

For professional-level talent, a summary will suffice. For job-seekers with only a few years of experience, a "headline" is a quick way to make an impact. The headline appears below your name, address, and contact information (never use your work email address).

For example:

- Award-winning graphic designer

- Marketing associate with experience running online and social media campaigns

- Communications manager for fast-growing Fortune 1000 company

- Biomechanical engineer with nanotechnology expertise

—

PROFESSIONAL EXPERIENCE AND ACCOMPLISHMENTS

The "professional experience" section is the bulk of your resume. It's a chronological listing (starting with the most recent and working backward) of every job you've had. If you've had 15 jobs in 25 years, list them all. The most detail, of course, will be devoted to your current position. In fact, your current job should account for about 75 percent of the detail of your professional experience. The only exception here is if your previous job has significant or different experience that you also want to showcase. If this is the case, you should also highlight your second job.

In addition, include a brief summary of your current responsibilities and contributions to the goals and growth of the company. If a recruiter or hiring manager reads nothing else, they will understand your skill set, competencies, and ability to contribute in your next role.

By highlighting "select achievements," you can also provide more detail that substantiates the achievement and could prompt a "tell me more" question during an interview. One way to approach these accomplishments is to think about three stories you will want to tell an interviewer. These should be stories that quickly capture and convey your technical skills and your leadership capabilities—what you're good at.

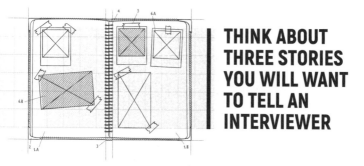

THINK ABOUT THREE STORIES YOU WILL WANT TO TELL AN INTERVIEWER

Each story should have three parts: the circumstance or challenge, the action taken, and the result. Be specific, with numbers, percentages, and other quantifiable details. If your marketing plan contributed to a 34 percent increase in sales or if you led a team that improved operational efficiency by 57 percent, say it!

DIVISIONAL FINANCIAL CONTROLLER– COMMERCIAL PRODUCTS
(2014 to Present)

Controller ($XXX million in sales), reporting to president and dotted line to CFO.

Select Achievements
- Oversaw data analysis team in identifying $XX million of revenue leakage.
- Led reengineering projects in Latin America, resulting in $XX million in cost savings.
- Drove implementation of company-wide CRM process.

DIRECTOR, PLANING AND ANALYSIS
(2010 to 2014)

Created XX-person financial planning and analysis group.

Select Achievements
- Established company-wide strategic planning process, including annual operating plans and quarterly KPIs.
- Evaluated strategic alliances, including 2 completed acquisitions.

And remember, you did not accomplish everything by yourself. You were part of a team, whether as a leader or member. Saying "we" and "our team" does not dilute your impact. Rather, it strengthens you and shows that you really are a team player/leader who knows how to motivate, inspire, acknowledge, and celebrate others. This is far more effective than merely saying, "I am a team player."

—

YOUR EDUCATION

The longer it's been since you graduated, the further back your education will be listed on your resume. If you are a senior vice president who has worked for several multinational companies, the fact that you went to an Ivy League school is a plus, but it's not the only reason someone should hire you.

For a recent college graduate, the opposite is true. Your education, internships, and significant educational experiences are what you want to showcase. Your resume will probably start with your college education and list internships or other notable experiences at the top. Your job experience (such as summer jobs) will probably be less important in terms of skills, but they should be listed because they show you have experience in the workplace.

—

FINAL NOTES FOR YOUR RESUME

PROFESSIONAL AFFILIATIONS AND AWARDS

List your association memberships, relevant positions you have held in these organizations, and any honors or awards you have received.

PERSONAL INFORMATION

Some people argue for including personal information; others say you should omit it. My advice is to be strategic about it. Just listing hobbies ("I enjoy reading and gardening") doesn't do much to distinguish you. But activities that say something about your traits should be included: You participate in competitive sports; you've finished multiple Ironman triathlons; you served in the Peace Corps; you're an accomplished cellist. If the information showcases a differentiating facet of yourself or what you bring to your next employer, then go for it.

REFERENCES

It is assumed that you have references, so it's not necessary to list them or say that they are "available upon request."

COVER LETTER

Yes, many people think they're not important anymore—especially in a tight job market when employers are clamoring to hire people. Why go through the effort? The advice here is to always write one—even when you're applying online and a cover letter is "optional." A cover letter is an important way to highlight who you are, why you are interested in a position, and why you should be considered for it. A cover letter also personalizes your communication, giving you the opportunity to express yourself as being enthusiastic about exploring this opportunity. In just a few sentences you can translate your background and experience into how you can satisfy the job requirements. Bottom line—can't hurt and may very well help.

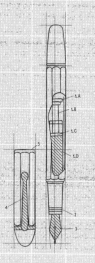

IN JUST A FEW SENTENCES YOU CAN TRANSLATE YOUR BACKGROUND AND EXPERIENCE INTO HOW YOU CAN SATISFY THE JOB REQUIREMENTS

YOUR ONLINE PRESENCE

That "funny" picture about that "crazy" time, which you (or your friends) posted on social media, can follow you right into your next job search. Increasingly, employers scour social media and more than half have found content that nixed a candidate from a job opportunity. And unfortunately, there's no "just kidding" button on social media.

It's a great irony: Social media goes a long way toward helping you find a job, but it can just as easily cost you the job you want. You won't even know it happened since your digital missteps take you out of the running before you get into the interview.

In other words, what happens in Vegas really doesn't stay there.

Probably it was just a joke or meant to be private. But we should all ask ourselves: Is anything private? Know what's out there! Google yourself: Type in your name and see what comes up. You'll instantly be reminded how easily your past follows you and how effortlessly an HR department or hiring manager can uncover something you'd prefer not to be their first impression.

—

TWEETING YOURSELF TO A JOB

Your ever-present smartphone makes it so easy to post, tweet, comment—instantly, before you've had time to think twice about it. But do think twice about it. Here are some tips:

• POST WITH NO REGRETS

"Will I offend someone? How can this come back to haunt me?" These two questions can prevent so much anguish. And it's not just athletes or celebrities who get themselves into trouble over controversial tweets and posts. And, don't be fooled into thinking there is some kind of "wall" between sites such as Facebook, Instagram, and Twitter, and the largely professional ones such as LinkedIn. Your online presence is one entity— your digital brand—and your next employer is looking everywhere.

• CHOOSE POSITIVITY OVER NEGATIVITY

Most of the time, it's better to follow your grandma's advice: "If you don't have something nice to say, don't say it." Now, I'm not suggesting you have to be wallpaper, but most of us respond much better to grace and dignity than to negativity. There's only one road: Take the high road.

IF YOU DON'T HAVE SOMETHING NICE TO SAY, DON'T SAY IT

WASH, RINSE, REPEAT

On a regular basis "wash, rinse, and repeat" your social media brand to ensure it's still relevant— and just to make sure there isn't a picture, post, or tweet made years before that shouldn't be there.

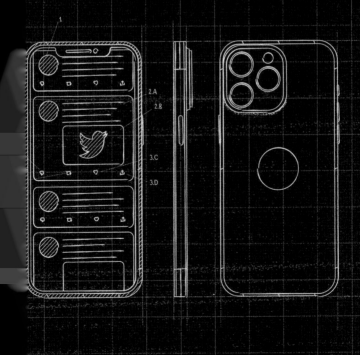

LINKEDIN: A MUST-HAVE PROFILE

When I'm reviewing a candidate's background, one of the first things I typically do is check the person's resume against their LinkedIn profile. I'm looking for consistency and more details. Sometimes the wording is different, but I want to see the same jobs, titles, and basic information. Gaps, different time frames, and inconsistent information are red flags to me, signaling either a problem with the resume or the way the person is trying to present themselves online.

Here is a brief overview of some of the ways you can elevate your online presence.

• YOUR PHOTO

Choose one that projects confidence and approachability. Use a recent photo you genuinely like. As long as you project professionalism, it doesn't matter if the photo was taken in a studio on your back patio or in your living room by a friend with an iPhone. Once you post the picture, ask a few friends to take a look. Is it clear? In focus? What's the first word that comes to mind when they look at the picture?

• YOUR INTRODUCTORY TITLE

Imagine someone has just asked you, "What do you do?" Your brief reply might be, "I'm the vice president of manufacturing for XYZ Global." Or you might say, "I bring next-generation products from design into the marketplace." Both are correct. But which is more effective for you? The answer is, it depends. If you work for the leader in your field—a Fortune 100 company, the hot digital startup, a top-tier institution—you may want to showcase your official job title as the introductory title of your LinkedIn profile. For example, many large company senior executives use their current title and company name because, for them, that says it all. The other school of thought says to use a short description to convey not only what you do, but how you do it: delivering patient-centered health care (versus head of nursing); connecting great people with jobs they love (versus head of talent acquisition); helping people and organizations tell their story and distinguish themselves in the marketplace (versus public relations professional). Once intrigued, recruiters, hiring managers, and others can glance down a few lines to read your current job title.

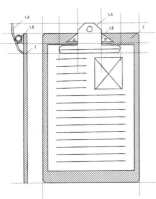

RECRUITERS, HIRING MANAGERS, AND OTHERS CAN GLANCE DOWN A FEW LINES

• YOUR SUMMARY

This is your "elevator pitch," your sixty-second wrap-up in three to four sentences. Just like an entrepreneur "pitching" a startup, or a writer trying to introduce a screenplay to a producer, you have an idea to sell. That idea is you! Rather than trying to tweak your summary every time you're pursuing a job, go all out writing one summary while keeping these basics in mind:

- Use First-Person Pronouns: It's okay to say "I"—people expect to hear from you directly. Referring to yourself in third person—"John is an experienced..." "Mary is a talented..."—sounds awkward and undermines the connection you're trying to make.

- Make It Meaningful to Others: While the content of your summary statement makes it all about you, the connection it makes is all about others. In a short amount of space and without too many words, you are showcasing who you are and what you bring to your next employer. Keep the audience in mind as you write your summary statement, particularly if you're looking to attract recruiters and hiring managers.

—

SUMMARY

WHILE THE CONTENT OF YOUR SUMMARY STATEMENT MAKES IT ALL ABOUT YOU, THE CONNECTION IT MAKES IS ALL ABOUT OTHERS

YOUR EXPERIENCE

Just as with your resume, you should use an accomplishment-first approach when presenting your experience in your LinkedIn profile. In fact, a great way to start building your profile is to literally cut and paste from your resume.

If you're among the many professionals who haven't addressed their LinkedIn profile in years, or if you are creating one for the first time, don't try to do everything at once. Start with what you have. You can leverage your resume to fill out the experience section. Use bullet points to list three to five accomplishments from your current job. Name the accomplishment and the result. For your past jobs, use the same approach, highlighting your top accomplishments.

Your next revision should move beyond what you've accomplished to how you did it. How did you lead that team of colleagues? What were the key points of launching that new product line? Post videos, blogs, and more. Maybe you participated on a panel at a virtual industry conference or gave a speech on a topic about which you have a great deal of expertise, and the event was recorded and shared online. Or perhaps you wrote a blog about a topic that's meaningful to you, or an article that ran on an industry website. Share these external links that showcase your expertise. They will enliven and enrich your profile.

As you achieve new accomplishments, add new bullet points and remove older ones. When possible, include links to the product you launched or a presentation you gave. By updating your profile (and your resume at the same time), you'll also show the progression in your skills and experiences.

—

LINKS AND LOGOS

The beauty of an online platform such as LinkedIn is that it allows you to link easily to your current and former employers, as well as to products and even specific projects that you've worked on. For example, let's say you currently work for a well-recognized consumer company. By including the company logo and a link to its LinkedIn page, your profile becomes more visually appealing and more dynamic. Even if a recruiter or hiring manager spends no more than five seconds scanning your LinkedIn profile, a well-recognized logo will make an impact.

Conversely, let's say you work for a small startup, one that's not recognizable. When you include a link to that company's LinkedIn page or "About Us" section on its website, you provide an instant resource for a recruiter or hiring manager to find out more.

The same goes for the education section of your profile. If your alma mater is a well-known institution, using its logo will leverage the school's "brand recognition." It will also make a visual connection with others who attended that school. You'd be surprised how much weight this carries when building your network.

Finally, links and logos can also enhance the impact of the personal interests that you list in your profile. If you volunteer with Habitat for Humanity, or your first job out of college was with Teach for America, or you had an interesting internship at a well-known nonprofit or institution, that entity's logo and link add visual and dynamic appeal to your profile.

—

RECOMMENDATIONS AND ENDORSEMENTS

LinkedIn's features for collecting recommendations and endorsements can help you build credibility. This is especially true with recommendations and less so with endorsements, which are done literally with the click of a button.

How much thought goes into that? LinkedIn has beefed up its endorsement process by noting when someone who is recognized as being highly skilled in a particular area endorses someone else. For example, your profile might show that in the category of social media, five people who are highly skilled endorse you. Such "expert" endorsements are thought to carry more weight because of the assumption that these are people who can really attest to your level of expertise.

THE MOST POWERFUL ENDORSEMENT IS THE ONE WRITTEN BY A GENUINELY ENTHUSED PERSON

Occasionally, a client or former or current colleague will write an unprompted recommendation (for your review and approval). But most of the time, you'll have to ask for recommendations from bosses, mentors, colleagues, and clients. While many people fall into the quid pro quo of "you recommend me and I'll recommend you," be careful that not every laudatory comment has a twin some place. The most powerful endorsement is the one written by a genuinely enthused person whose expectations you exceeded. It doesn't matter how high up in the organization that person is. A thoughtful, well-written recommendation written by a peer who speaks with some specifics can do more to distinguish your profile than generic comments from people who are many levels above you.

—

A LIVING DOCUMENT

Your resume isn't an epitaph, focused on the past. Rather, your resume should be approached as a living document that, when coupled with your LinkedIn profile, can generate real enthusiasm.

Taking this approach accomplishes two important goals. First, a real-time resume helps you capture an expanded role or new accomplishments while they're still fresh in your mind. Did you finish the past year 12 percent above plan? Update your resume to reflect that fact. Have you just been assigned to launch a marketing campaign for a new product line? Capture that in a few sentences on your resume.

Second, your living-document approach reminds you to keep your LinkedIn profile or other professional media presence updated and relevant. Then, when recruiters, hiring managers, or anyone else checks you out online, they'll see the latest information about you.

Then, as calling card and introduction combined, your resume and your online presence will help you open the door to the next opportunities.

—

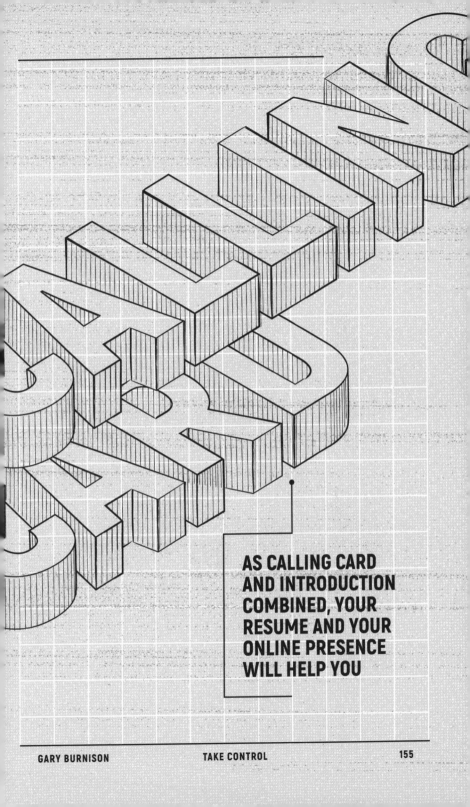

AS CALLING CARD
AND INTRODUCTION
COMBINED, YOUR
RESUME AND YOUR
ONLINE PRESENCE
WILL HELP YOU

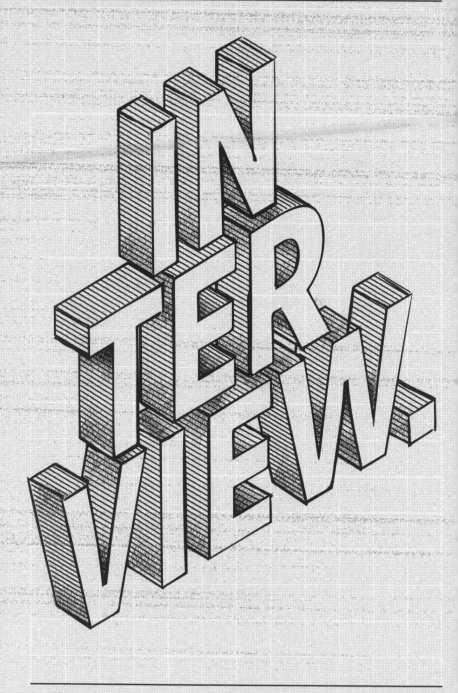

TAKE CONTROL

Chapter 6

THE INTERVIEW – ON SCREEN, IN PERSON

No matter how many job interviews someone has been on, or how well they think on their feet, the unfortunate truth is that most people rarely are as prepared as they could be. In fact, of all the questions I'm asked related to the job search process, "how to ace an interview" is by far the one I hear most often. This is as true among seasoned professionals as it is for those entering the workforce.

We all can get nervous when faced with the unknown— and particularly involving something we want. We psych ourselves out and run the risk of doing something that doesn't present ourselves in the best light.

That's clearly what was happening to the man I saw at a corner table in a Starbucks. His leg was pumping up and

down as he shuffled
through notecards. I could
see his resume on the tabletop
from where I was standing.

"Job interview, huh?" I said
as I approached him.

He looked up, his eyes intense
with caffeine and desperation.
"Yeah, and I really need this job."

"Well, you're not doing yourself any
favors," I told him, pointing to his
triple red eye (coffee with three shots
of espresso). "The first thing you
need to do is take some deep breaths
and relax. It's an interview, not an
interrogation. So, treat this like a
conversation, pure and simple."

Then I asked him if he had a picture
on his phone that was special to him.

"My family," he said, showing me
the screen.

"That's what matters most—not this
job interview," I told him. "Think
about two hours from now, when the
interview is over and you're going

TREAT THIS LIKE A CONVER-SATION

home to see your family. You keep them in mind, and you'll have a great interview." And then I wished him good luck.

No matter if this is your first or second professional job out of college, or you're a senior executive who has been through the drill countless times, your emotions are bound to be mixed and intense—like the guy at Starbucks was experiencing. After all, most people approach interviews as a cross between a trip to Disneyland and a visit to the dentist to have a tooth extracted. On one hand, they look forward to it, but on the other they dread it. By letting their imaginations run wild, they amp up their panic until they cannot put two coherent sentences together—or else overcompensate by talking nonstop.

Relax, you've got this. An interview isn't an audition for a Broadway play. While you should know your lines, learning them is not the first thing to do. The goal is to have a free-flowing exchange with the interviewer(s) so you can get to know them, and they can get to know you. You can quell your fears with the right mindset and thorough preparation—and that's what this chapter aims to do for you.

In this chapter, we will look at interviewing at every stage: from your interview prep, through the actual interview, and into the follow-up and beyond—all with a focus on how you can authentically showcase who you are, what you bring to this next opportunity, and how to determine if this is the right move for you.

—

WE NEVER GET OUT OF SIXTH GRADE

For most of us, there is a deep emotional current running through the entire interview process: We never really get out of sixth grade. Think about it: Back when we were 11 or 12 years old, our biggest worries were whether the other kids were going to like us. Would they want us on their team? Will they share what they have or what they know? Now tell me, has any of this changed, especially in the context of the interview process?

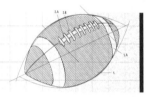

OF COURSE, YOU WANT TO BE ACCEPTED, TO BE PICKED FOR THE TEAM, AND TO WIN

Looking at an interview in this way can lead to an *aha* moment that helps you understand your feelings and why you feel so uncomfortable and vulnerable. Of course, you want to be accepted, to be picked for the team, and to win. And most fundamental of all, you want to be liked. The good news is, with self-awareness of your emotions and preparation for the interview, you can increase your chances of connecting with others and having a successful interview.

—

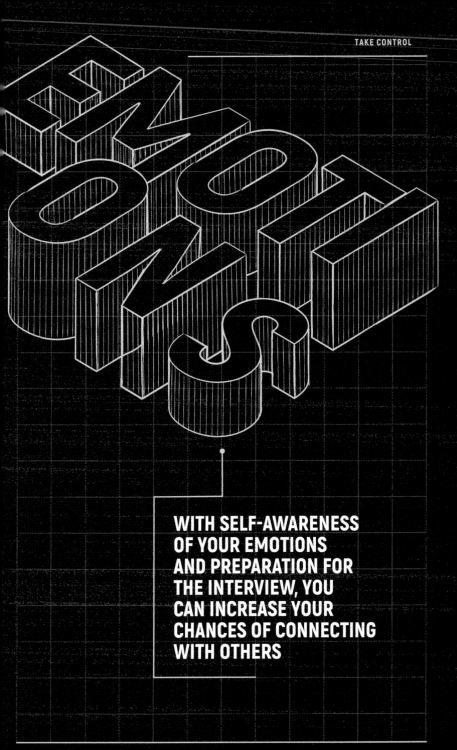

EMOTIONS

WITH SELF-AWARENESS OF YOUR EMOTIONS AND PREPARATION FOR THE INTERVIEW, YOU CAN INCREASE YOUR CHANCES OF CONNECTING WITH OTHERS

MAKING THE MOST OF THE FIRST SEVEN SECONDS

Unfortunately, most people form an impression of others within seven seconds. During that brief time, an interviewer will make crucial determinations about you, including your likability, your trustworthiness, how aggressive or passive you seem, and how well you would fit in with others on the team.

Based on this initial determination (typically unconsciously), an interviewer will decide (probably also unconsciously) whether to help you in the interview—by rephrasing questions, giving helpful feedback, assuring you with verbal and nonverbal cues—or not. Unfair? Yes. But human nature being what it is, that's how this usually works. Knowing that, you can ensure your preparation makes all the difference.

—

YOUR INTERVIEW PREP

As obvious as it might sound, it's surprising how many people under-prepare for interviews. Top of the list: thinking they can just "wing it"—without preparing sound bites, such as their three top accomplishments. To avoid that misstep, here are five things to do to help you prepare for the big job interview:

01 LEARN ABOUT THE COMPANY'S STORY, PRODUCTS, AND SERVICES

People miss this one all the time. They go into an interview without a strong understanding of what the company does. Just knowing the basics isn't enough. Learn all you can about the company—its history, leadership team, current successes, and challenges. If possible, try out the company's products and services, and talk to people who use them. Greater knowledge about the company's customers will also help you present your skills and experiences in context. You'll appear more relevant to the hiring manager. And the more relevant you are, the better the connection you'll make.

02 RESEARCH WHOM YOU'RE GOING TO MEET AND PREPARE SOME ICEBREAKERS

When your interview is arranged, ask for the names and titles of everyone you're going to speak with. You can even ask the interview coordinator if there is anything you should know about these people. But don't stop there. Look them up on LinkedIn and find out more about their backgrounds. You're looking for connection points, such as having worked at the same company several years ago. Even small things you notice can help you come up with some icebreakers. Look for current themes—maybe the company just announced a new product, or the CEO was recently on television with positive news about the company. Even a benign observation—"I see that the company just made an acquisition. This must be a very exciting and busy time"—can be an effective opener and conversation starter.

03 FIND OUT MORE ABOUT HOW WORK GETS DONE

A big question to ask is how the company approaches in-person, remote, or hybrid work. One way is to inquire about the company's experience with remote work—its policies, expectations, and flexibility. There are many questions you can ask about how the nature of work evolved over the past few years that will make you sound relevant and engaged, while also sharing your own perspective and experiences.

04 PICK THE RIGHT CLOTHES AND DO A "MIRROR CHECK"

This applies equally to online and in-person interviews. Plan your outfit ahead of time—try it on and make sure that it's clean, pressed, and still fits. Even if you're head and shoulders on camera, make sure you dress head to toe. You'll not only feel more professional, but if you need to move (for example, getting up to shut the door that your dog just nosed open) you won't reveal that you're wearing gym shorts with that shirt and blazer.

05 DO A BACK-GROUND CHECK

As in *your* background—for an online interview that is. While Zoom, Team, and Meet are all part of the fabric of our daily lives, take extra care for interviews. Do a camera setup with a friend to scour the background: clean, neat, and no distracting items in view (like that pile of dirty laundry visible through an open doorway behind you). You can also test out a virtual background that masks your environment; for example, if your Zoom room is also your bedroom. You might want to pick one that mimics an office space or another neutral background that doesn't distract from you. Once again, test out the background with a friend ahead of time to make sure it sends the right message—and that you don't appear to be a disembodied head floating in a virtual scene.

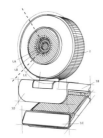

TEST OUT THE BACKGROUND WITH A FRIEND AHEAD OF TIME

THE BEST ADVICE

You know what you want to say during the interview. But what you can never be sure of is what the interviewer will ask. Some questions will be the standards, such as "What are your strengths?" Others could range from zingers that stump you to the bizarre—"If you were an animal, what would you be?"

Here's the best advice I know for preparing yourself. Use your smartphone to video record yourself (or have someone else do it) as you answer interview questions (there's a list of them on the following pages). When you play back the recording, listen to your answers. How can you say it more concisely, bringing your response down to a tight 30-second answer? You need responses that are punchy, crisp, compelling, and to the point. In the other extreme, one-word answers do you no favors. But neither will a filibuster—like a candidate who came in for a 30-minute interview and talked nonstop for 20 minutes on the first question. Make a point and be economical with words. You can always elaborate later when the interviewer asks a follow-up question.

And it's not just what you say—it's also how you say it. As you watch the video recording of yourself, be aware of your nonverbal cues and what they say to your interviewer. For example, making eye contact (yes, even on Zoom) will help you appear more confident and friendlier. Keep your hands free to gesture. Lean forward, but don't be on the edge of your seat. And smile!

Conveying happiness and confidence will help you forge a connection, while also making others feel good about themselves.

—

THE QUESTIONS YOU NEED TO ANSWER

Here are some questions you should be prepared to answer. You may not be asked these exact questions but preparing answers for them will help you handle almost anything you are asked.

- ## WHAT HAVE YOU LEARNED THE MOST FROM THESE LAST FEW YEARS?

  Even if this is not asked directly, you will want to share your response to this one as part of the interview. This is a perfect opportunity to show your agility and adaptability, especially when managing ambiguity. Think about it: For the past few years we've been in a constant state of flux. The good news is, we've all built new capabilities, perhaps without realizing it. We've become comfortable with being uncomfortable. We've learned what to do when we didn't know what to do, amid circumstances and challenges we had never experienced before. And that's a great story to tell.

• WHAT HAVE YOU BEEN WORKING ON?

It's the No. 1 interview question I like to ask. I'm looking for clues that tell me how the words on someone's resume translate into today's reality. It provides context.

• TELL ME ABOUT YOURSELF.

When it comes to answering this old standard, too many people respond by regurgitating their resume. That's not what your interviewer wants to hear. Rather, this is an opening to help the interviewer get to know you, beyond what's on your resume. We all have a story to tell—something that we're passionate about, a challenge we've faced, or even an interesting fact about ourselves. Just talk for about 30 seconds—brevity is everything with this one. Then let the interviewer respond. Now, you've made it a conversation.

• DESCRIBE A SITUATION IN WHICH YOU TOOK INITIATIVE TO ACCOMPLISH A GOAL.

Your interviewer is listening for examples of how you've been proactive and results driven. Describe your motivation and how you used your creativity to solve a problem or identify an opportunity.

TAKE A RISK TO GET PERSONAL

"Tell me about yourself" is an invitation for you to share a very short anecdote or some brief personal information about your life outside of work. I've heard people talk about everything from being a world-class sushi chef to an ice carver.

Share a story that makes you memorable. Everyone has something to share.

The challenge, though, is that many people are so eager to show off the work projects they've been involved in, they don't take a risk to get personal.

SHARE A STORY THAT MAKES YOU MEMORABLE

• WHAT VALUE DO YOU BRING?

This can be a tough one because it's so vague. The key here is to pick two or three main qualifications for the job and explain how you meet them. For more junior positions, you'll want to spend more time talking about your technical skills. But if you're further in your career, then focus on highlighting how you manage, work with, motivate, and engage with others.

• WHAT IS YOUR GREATEST CAREER ACCOMPLISHMENT?

This is one of the most important questions to prepare for. Giving a great answer can help you land the job. Just don't drag on too long; tell a quick story with specific details (which is why the videorecording exercise is so helpful). Choose an accomplishment that is most relevant to the position you're applying for. And make sure to quantify the accomplishment: Did you help reduce expenses? Increase productivity or revenue? Even something that gave the company higher recognition in its industry counts.

CHOOSE AN ACCOMPLISHMENT THAT IS MOST RELEVANT TO THE POSITION YOU'RE APPLYING FOR

• WHAT ARE YOUR WEAKNESSES?

Saying that you "work too hard" or you "care too much" won't cut it. You need to give a real answer that shows your self-awareness. After all, self-awareness precedes self-change and self-improvement. Prepare a couple of examples of areas you're working on where you know you need to improve—and what you're doing about it.

• WHAT MAJOR PROBLEM, CHALLENGE, OR FAILURE HAVE YOU HAD TO OVERCOME? HOW DID YOU DO IT?

In your response, you can highlight your skills and competencies, but also your perseverance, work ethic, personal commitment, and integrity. Overcoming numerous or significant difficulties to succeed requires these qualities. Demonstrate your resilience by getting real about the challenges you've overcome.

• WHY DO YOU WANT TO WORK HERE?

This is an opportunity to show how much you know about the company and why you believe that you'd be a good fit. Describe what you admire about the company—its mission and purpose, products and services. Be passionate—talk about what you'd like to learn and why.

—

BE A GUEST - IT'S NOT ABOUT YOU

Now that you've invested time and energy in your interview prep, you have greatly increased your chances of success. Not only do you know what to say, but you've also rehearsed how you're going to say it—with purpose and passion. But here's the thing about the interview itself. It isn't about you. It's all about the hiring manager, the other team members, and every other person you're going to meet—whether in person or virtually.

HERE'S THE THING ABOUT THE INTERVIEW ITSELF. IT ISN'T ABOUT YOU

It's like being a guest in someone's home for the first time. To show respect, and make a connection with your hosts, you follow the "house rules." In your interview, you follow the same visitor's protocol. This is especially important when you're meeting in person, but even virtually you need to be the gracious guest as you smile and make eye contact, listen carefully to others, and pay attention to their pace and tempo. You're reading the interviewer's tone and body language. If you're in sync with them, the exchange will feel much more relaxed, and the conversation will flow.

—

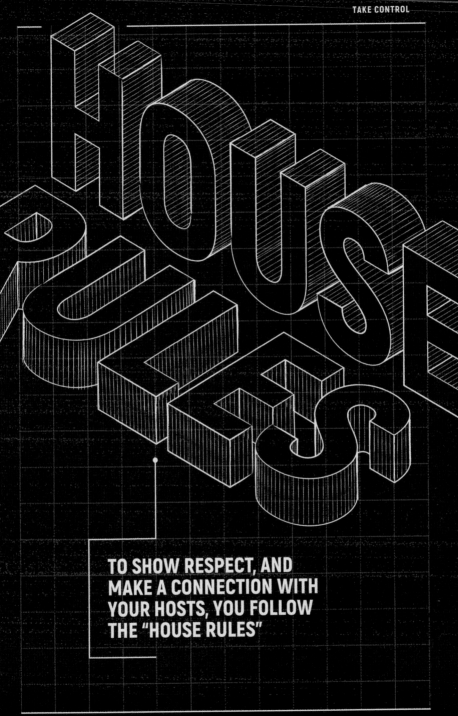

HOUSE RULES

TO SHOW RESPECT, AND
MAKE A CONNECTION WITH
YOUR HOSTS, YOU FOLLOW
THE "HOUSE RULES"

BE PREPARED TO BE ASSESSED

At some point in the process, it's highly likely that you'll be given an assessment. Employers today are using assessments to evaluate candidates and help ensure a good fit, especially for higher-level jobs.

At the entry level or in early phases of someone's careers, assessments will likely be automated. Most people generally accept being assessed as part of the process for getting a job they really want. The only complaint is that applicants too often don't see the results. All they know is whether they ultimately get invited for an interview or not.

For more senior positions, assessments tend to be higher touch evaluations. The objective is to identify the candidate's strengths, areas where they need more development, and how they will fit with the overall organization. And it doesn't stop there. After being hired, people are often assessed as part of their ongoing career development—and that's a very good thing. Each assessment is a reflection of where they are at any given stage of their career and how they are evolving.

After all, to have the careers we want, we all need to work on our game. It's like in basketball, where the best players spend hours every day practicing free throws so that, when the game is on the line, they can make the shot. Your "free throws" will be those things you need to work on—the skills you need to build. If your current or prospective employer wants to assess you, don't fight it! Assessments are a gift of clear, objective feedback on where you are and the potential you can develop as you keep working on your game.

—

THE THREE STAGES OF THE INTERVIEW

An interview normally goes through three basic stages: opening, middle, and close. Let's take a look at each.

—

THE OPENING: AN INSTANT CONNECTION

Your interview begins with the first encounter. Online, that means exhibiting a friendly demeanor and greeting others as they appear on screen. In person, it starts with your entrance into the building or corporate campus. Everyone—the parking lot attendant, the security guard, the receptionist—is part of your interview experience.

I've heard many stories of candidates who were rude to the receptionist, which was reason enough for them not to be asked back for a second interview. I also know the opposite: When a candidate was polite and respectful as she chatted with a custodian adjusting a vent in the waiting room near the CEO's office. Later in the day, the custodian made it a point tell the CEO, "The woman who came in this morning was so nice—very interesting and easy to talk to." And the CEO took that "recommendation" seriously.

Once your interview gets underway, an initial period is typically devoted to establishing rapport. This is an opportunity for you to show your authenticity, confidence, poise, and professional presence. In your words and actions, you show that you are genuinely interested in getting to know others—even more than you are interested in selling your skills, experience, and accomplishments.

IN YOUR WORDS AND ACTIONS, YOU SHOW THAT YOU ARE GENUINELY INTERESTED IN GETTING TO KNOW OTHERS

During this initial period, notice the surroundings. In person, you may see a trinket or picture in the hiring manager's office that catches your eye. It's an easy and good-natured connection to make. On screen, it may be harder to see the person's background, but something might stand out. And if your research into the interviewer's background revealed a commonality, this is the time to mention it.

—

THE MID-STAGE:
YOUR CONTRIBUTION

The middle of the interview is the main event: the exchange of information about the way your background fits the company's needs. You and the interviewer engage in a give-and-take conversation in which you learn about each other. You demonstrate how you can contribute to the achievement of the organization's goals, while you also find out more about the position. The manager has specific goals that must be achieved. Your objective in the interview is to show exactly how you can help achieve them.

—

THE QUIRKY
QUESTION

Somewhere in the mid-stage of the interview, you might get lobbed a totally unexpected question. How many basketballs would it take to fill a room? How many quarters would it take to reach the top of a 10-story building? Hearing such a quirky query, you might wonder what is going on!

The interviewer isn't looking for the correct answer. Rather, the purpose is to probe your reactions, to see how you adapt to the unexpected. Most important, the interviewer wants to find out more about how you think.

THE INTERVIEWER WANTS TO FIND OUT MORE ABOUT HOW YOU THINK

Like the tuna fish sandwich test. I have asked this question in the middle of an interview: "How do you make a tuna fish sandwich?"

I've been greeted with cold stares and even complaints: "Why would you ask me that?" But other people get into it: sharing how they make a tuna fish sandwich or, better yet, asking how I like my sandwich—mayo, no mayo; relish, no relish; etc. If you are asked one of these questions, turn it into a dialogue. Ask questions. Make it a collaborative effort, not an IQ test.

People who can handle the unexpected question—and use it to showcase who they are and how they think—are more likely to be adaptable and curious. And those are key components of an extremely important quality: learning agility, which is so important, our firm views it as the No. 1 predictor of success. Learning agility is defined as the ability and willingness to take past experiences and lessons learned and apply them to new and first-time challenges. Or, as I like to call it—knowing what to do when you don't know what to do.

—

"DO YOU HAVE QUESTIONS FOR ME?"

At some point during the interview, the hiring manager is going to ask, "What questions do you have for me?" You'll want to show your preparation and engagement by asking questions that are smart and strategic. For example, ask more about the job responsibilities or how the department functions.

The questions you ask aren't just to get more information. They should also show the interviewer how you think. By easily inserting your questions into the interview, you'll turn a one-way question-and-answer session into a conversation.

THE QUESTIONS YOU ASK AREN'T JUST TO GET MORE INFORMATION

THE INTERVIEW CLOSE

The discussion will begin to wind down as the interviewer starts summarizing or perhaps volunteers a little information about "next steps"—for example, meeting other team members. It's important to restate, in short fashion, your interest in and enthusiasm for the job. Summarize why you think you're a good fit for the organization. Ask interviewers if there is anything else they would like to know about you or that you can elaborate on. Is there anything from the conversation that you can clarify? Do they have any questions about anything you said that you can answer now? Finish strong by showing your interest in the position and your enthusiasm for the company, in your tone and with your body language.

—

FINISH STRONG BY SHOWING YOUR INTEREST IN THE POSITION AND YOUR ENTHUSIASM FOR THE COMPANY

THE TOP 10 THINGS INTERVIEWERS ARE LOOKING FOR

01 CULTURE FIT

The sense that you would work well with others in the company, department, or team

02 MOTIVATION

What drives you to succeed

03 SKILLS

Mostly technical skills for junior positions; management and leadership skills for more experienced executives

04 LEADERSHIP POTENTIAL

How you lead yourself and others; your ability to be groomed for a leadership position one day

HOW YOU LEAD YOURSELF AND OTHERS

05 COMMUNICATION SKILLS

Your speaking and listening abilities

06 POISE AND APPEARANCE

How you present yourself; how customers or clients will experience you

07 PROBLEM-SOLVING SKILLS

How adept you are at finding a solution by looking beyond the obvious or what's already been done

HOW ADEPT YOU ARE AT FINDING A SOLUTION BY LOOKING BEYOND THE OBVIOUS

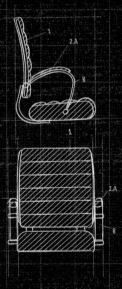

08 INTERPERSONAL SKILLS

How you interact with others, how you make them feel

09 WILLINGNESS TO ACCEPT RESPONSIBILITY

How you respond when you're tasked with trying to create the "new and different," and "failing fast" is to be expected

HOW YOU RESPOND WHEN YOU'RE TASKED WITH TRYING TO CREATE THE "NEW AND DIFFERENT"

10 WORKING WELL UNDER PRESSURE

Being able to handle workplace stress without losing your cool

SAYING THANK YOU IN THE VIRTUAL WORLD

It's standard practice to send a note to your interviewers, thanking them for the opportunity and reiterating your interest in the position. The conventional wisdom is that it should always be a handwritten note. And, indeed, that is a great follow-up with a personalized touch.

But in these days of virtual working and interviewing, you're probably going to send that note by email. Just make sure you take as much time and care composing that email as you would writing on your best stationery.

THE NEXT STEPS

If you are going to be called back for additional interviews, you will typically find out soon. It will probably take the hiring manager a week or more to meet with other candidates and decide who among you will advance to the next round.

In the meantime, don't put your life on hold. Continue your networking; keep pursuing other opportunities and talking to other companies. If you are called back, you will likely meet with other members of the team—and be prepared for multiple rounds of interviews.

As the selection process continues, you may be given an assignment. For example, you could be asked to provide your thoughts about the role or the strategy. You may have to present a written document, make a presentation, or both.

Don't be surprised if you meet with a team member who is more junior than you are. Often this is a way to probe culture fit. This is the Golden Rule: Treat everyone the way you wish to be treated and you'll never go wrong.

One of the biggest challenges of multiple interviews is keeping things fresh for yourself. It's natural to begin to wonder, didn't I say that already? I remember this feeling from my days in investment banking, when I was part of a road-show team doing investor presentations. Sometimes we'd meet with eight different investment groups in one day, fly at night to the next city, and start all over again in the morning. No matter that it was repetitive for us, we had to make each presentation seem as if it was the one and only.

The same applies when you're in the third or fourth (or more) round of interviews. Don't think you can skip the preamble because the various interviewers have already traded notes. When interviewer No. 6 asks you, "So, tell me about yourself," smile and answer the question like it's the first time you're telling it.

—

HOW TO WORK WITH OTHERS

Chapter 7

THE 4 CAREER KNOCKOUT PUNCHES

Job after job, one opportunity to the next ....
But where, exactly, are you headed? You must
have a plan—not only for where you want to
go, but even more important for the skills and
experiences you'll need to gain along the way.
Otherwise, you could make a hasty, wrong move
that turns your career path into a careen path.

With every job you take, you need to ensure that you're
accelerating your learning and development—more
knowledge, new skills, and deeper experiences. No
matter what field you're in, there are four key areas that
are crucial to your advancement. Each is so important,
I call them "knockout punches." Possess them, and you'll
be a knockout in any job. Fail to develop them, and ...
well, you might be left staggering in your career.

—

THE 4 CAREER KNOCKOUT PUNCHES

01 DEALING WITH AMBIGUITY

W e've been in a constant state of flux—
and that's not going to change any time
soon. Making things even more complicated,
studies show that 90 percent of the problems
confronting managers and people in higher
positions are ambiguous—neither the problem
nor the solution is clear.

> ## SINCE AMBIGUITY ISN'T GOING AWAY, WE NEED TO DO MORE THAN JUST DEAL WITH IT

Since ambiguity isn't going away, we need to do more
than just deal with it. We actually should embrace
it. Otherwise, we run the risk of getting stuck. Here's
usually what happens: When circumstances are
ambiguous, we seek more information or dive into
every detail before making a decision or taking action.
Often, that only serves to further cloud the issue
because it looks like things could go in any number
of directions. Then we really don't know what to do.

Greater ambiguity raises the stakes for all of us to solve problems and make quality decisions. But here's the thing: as our firm's research shows, tough times can be a valuable proving ground—if you know how to find solutions, provide decisive direction, and tackle challenges. Add to that, the ability to expand your perspective and take the broadest view of an issue so you can make projections about the future (even though the future may be more uncertain than ever). Doing that repeatedly, and without having the total picture, is becoming a daily requirement, particularly as you advance in your career.

So how do you get there? It starts by letting go of the need for a clearcut "if/then" world where a distinct cause is immediately followed by a likely effect. Instead of wishing things were otherwise, it's time to go into the fog.

The clues to adopting this mental attitude can be found in the word, itself. "Ambi" derives from Latin, meaning both. So ambiguity really means things could possibly move in two (or more) directions. Same thing with ambivalence. It doesn't mean that we don't care—rather, we just feel equally strong in both directions.

Developing these skills takes time and practice. But the good news is, given today's complex challenges and fast-changing scenarios, you will have plenty of opportunity to exercise this skill and build the muscle of dealing with ambiguity. You'll be able to look in more than one direction so you can put in place a plan of action—along with a Plan B (or C...or D...) in case things change quickly.

"IN A PERFECT WORLD..."

How many times have we heard those words? What comes next is almost always a commentary of how things should be. But there is no perfect world—and futilely looking for one only makes everything else seem far worse by comparison.

This reminds us of the wise words of President Theodore Roosevelt: "Comparison is the thief of joy." We need to stop looking for some "perfect" solution and focus instead on what will work for us right now. Not a year from now, not six months, maybe not even next month. Today. That's the world we live in.

COMPARISON IS THE THIEF OF JOY

Granted, ambiguousness is probably not our favorite state of being—we much prefer clarity. But there's no avoiding the fact that today's new world in which we operate is still largely gray and unknown—and that probably won't change soon.

There will be plenty of times when you'll be making the best decision you can in the moment—until it's not a good decision anymore. As the saying goes, perfection is the enemy of good.

02 HANDLING AND MANAGING CHANGE

A s Charles Darwin observed: "It is not the strongest of the species that survives, it is the one that is most adaptable to change." Based on our firm's research (including assessments of 86 million professionals), we know that openness to change is a key indicator of performance and potential—especially when coupled with a willingness to experiment and the capability to learn from new experiences.

But let's be honest. Change is hard for most people.

The first step is to stop resisting change and get comfortable (or, at least, less uncomfortable) with it. This is the essence of having "change agility"—a key trait that allows us to move beyond "this is the way we've always done things."

So how do you do that? One way is to focus on the upside of change—seeing it as an opportunity to learn. For example, when a colleague suggests that's outside of "what we've always done," listen to the rationale. Instead of asking "why," embrace the possibility with "why not!"

The ability to navigate change starts with how you think—and, as our firm's experts tell us, three mindsets can help:

• 01. PURPOSE MINDSET

Purpose is more than just an organization's mission and values. It can help you become more open, deliberate, and consistent in how you manage change in the pursuit of an overarching purpose. As research shows, a strong sense of purpose also leads to greater engagement and more motivation—all of which contribute to navigating change.

• 02. COURAGE MINDSET

To harness the power of change, we all need to adopt a courageous mindset. Courage is also contagious, encouraging others around us to think in bigger and braver ways. The challenge, however, is that developing courage often means taking risks, which leads to the potential for loss or failure. But with courage, you can "fail fast and learn faster"—enabling you to become more agile and innovative.

• 03. INTEGRATIVE THINKING MINDSET

In the midst of change, integrative thinking helps us connect what's happening in one place (for example, our team, our department) to the entire

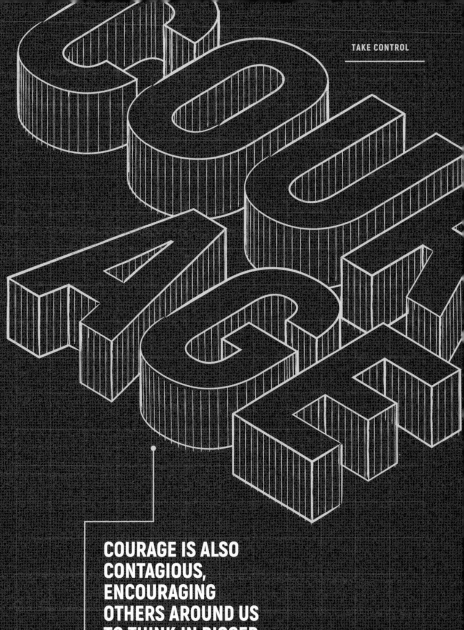

COURAGE IS ALSO
CONTAGIOUS,
ENCOURAGING
OTHERS AROUND US
TO THINK IN BIGGER
AND BRAVER WAYS

organization. The challenge, however, is this horizontal thinking goes against the traditional view, which is vertical, hierarchical, and siloed. The more you can look beyond one area, and instead adopt a holistic mindset, the better equipped you will become to navigate change— while making decisions in the moment.

03 MASTERING A FASTER PACE

ANTICIPATING AND NAVIGATING CHANGE

I can remember sitting down with the late Warren Bennis, a well-respected leadership guru who advised CEOs and U.S. presidents alike. He explained to me that the key to anticipating the change ahead is to accurately perceive the reality of today. We don't need to be visionaries; we just need to be grounded in what's really happening today—because that's the starting point for tomorrow.

"*I'm busy all the time.*" It's a mantra we're probably hearing (and saying) more frequently these days.

With so much to do, we think the answer is to keep moving faster. But mastering a faster pace is about more than mere acceleration. Rather, it's about moving at the optimal pace—after all, strategy is not only direction but, as important, velocity.

Mastering a faster pace also involves knowing when to push pause—even for just a moment—to regroup and recharge. We're like trapeze artists, flying through the air. But even in that moment of being completely ungrounded, we need to pause so we can reach for the next bar. Indeed, a little rest and perspective can go a long way toward helping us pick up the pace when necessary.

Our colleague Kevin Cashman, Global Leader of CEO & Executive Development, wrote about the value of "stepping back to lead forward" in his book, *The Pause Principle*. As Kevin wrote, "What sleep is to the mind and body, pause is to leadership and innovation. Pause transforms management into leadership and the status quo into new realities. Pause, the natural capability to step back in order to move forward with greater clarity, momentum, and impact, holds the creative power to reframe and refresh how we see ourselves and our relationships, our challenges, our capacities, our organizations, and missions within a larger context."

This does not mean slowing down. But it does mean pausing occasionally to reflect and accurately assess today's ever-changing reality. Then, after that brief pause, we will have greater understanding that helps us see what lies ahead—and how fast we need to move to get there.

We reflect ... Reflection is the only way to become our better selves—as we learn and grow. We reflect on who we are and who we want to become. That's how we paint a vision for our careers. Self-awareness always precedes self-change and self-improvement.

We reset ... When our circuit breakers get tripped, it's time for a reset—starting with our mindset. We leave behind what we've done in the past and imagine how we can do even better. But imagining, alone does not suffice. We find tangible ways to put our vision into action.

We are renewed ... As long as we are alive, we are always evolving. But as we contemplate just how far our careers have come, we can see more clearly how we have grown and developed. And at every step of the way, we roll with the punches.

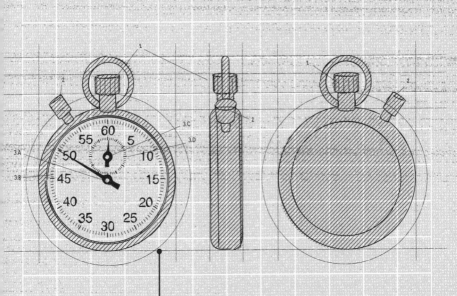

**AFTER THAT BRIEF
PAUSE, WE WILL HAVE
GREATER UNDERSTANDING
THAT HELPS US SEE
WHAT LIES AHEAD—AND
HOW FAST WE NEED TO
MOVE TO GET THERE**

04 CROSS-CULTURAL AGILITY

While the form may change; the substance remains the same: maintaining an inclusive mindset to compete in a marketplace that is somewhat borderless, yet heavily influenced by local nuance. That means dealing with different languages, cultural norms, business rules, and geopolitical tensions.

The secret of success is fostering an inclusive mindset. Inclusion is a behavior. Inclusion fully leverages and values different perspectives and backgrounds to drive results. Diversity is a fact. Differences make each person unique. Engagement is an emotion. The emotional connection we have with each other unlocks discretionary energy. When we are fluent in the language of inclusion, we become culturally agile.

WHEN WE ARE FLUENT IN THE LANGUAGE OF INCLUSION, WE BECOME CULTURALLY AGILE

The more cross-cultural agility we have, the more we can connect with and even lead others. One way to think about this is to imagine that you are about to embark on a journey—leading 10,000 people on a cross-country trip by foot—from New York City to Santa Monica, California.

As you stand in Battery Park, at the southernmost tip of Manhattan, gathered around you are people from dozens of countries—different backgrounds, experiences, and perspectives. And your job is to lead this diverse group. You know that a solitary walker, putting in 10 hours a day, could cover those 2,800 miles in about 90 days. But your job is to make sure that everyone around you is included on the journey.

As you ponder the enormity of leading thousands of people on such a trek—physically moving them from here to there—you wonder how you will keep everyone motivated and aligned, leaving the familiar for the unknown, losing some people and gaining others...

This is the essence of leadership—whether you're leading a team of 5, 50, 500, 5,000, or even just yourself. It is all about helping others believe and turning that belief into reality. To do that, you need cross-cultural agility to help you meet people where they are and inspire them to move forward—together.

Finally, the destination is reached: the beach in Santa Monica. As satisfying as the end goal is, it's only one moment out of many. Indeed, every journey is an accumulation of many moments. The moments are what truly matter most—moments of journeying with others.

The more cross-cultural agility you develop on your career journey, the better you will be able to see and appreciate the rich mosaic of backgrounds, experiences, knowledge, and perspectives as a vast wealth to be tapped.

The four career knockout punches are never one and done. We are constantly building these important skills so we can take control of our careers and help ensure that we are gaining the exposure and experiences we need to advance. That's how we "knock out" any doubts that we can, indeed, do the job we've been given to do.

—

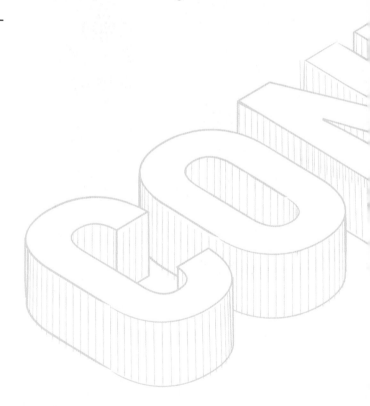

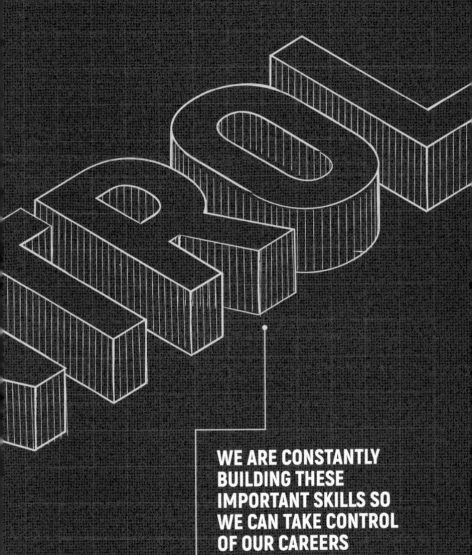

**WE ARE CONSTANTLY
BUILDING THESE
IMPORTANT SKILLS SO
WE CAN TAKE CONTROL
OF OUR CAREERS**

TAKE CONTROL

Chapter 8

GETTING ALONG WITH YOUR BOSS AND YOUR COWORKERS

We are not solo performers—poets in a garret, writing by candlelight, or sculptors working alone in the studio, chipping away at a block of marble. That's not the way we work, especially in today's collaborative world. We need others—and they need us.

Let's be honest, though. Interpersonal relationships are challenging, and group dynamics can amplify the challenges exponentially. To illustrate, let's imagine that you and a group of colleagues are going out for dinner. It's after six, and everyone is hungry. Standing on the sidewalk, you're trying to decide as a group where to go—Italian,

Asian, Southwestern, seafood, burgers, vegetarian … all those personal tastes and preferences—otherwise known as self-interest. How on earth can everyone come together around the shared interest of a meal together? It would be an interesting exercise, to say the least.

WE COME TOGETHER FROM DIFFERENT BACKGROUNDS, EXPERIENCES, PREFERENCES, AND PERSONALITIES

And yet, that's exactly what happens every day in the workplace. We come together from different backgrounds, experiences, preferences, and personalities. Now add pressure, stress, deadlines, and an ever-increasing pace of change.

To harness that energy as a force multiplier for good, we cannot stay polarized from each other. It's up to us to find a way to get along with others—especially our bosses and our coworkers.

—

ENERGY

TO HARNESS THAT ENERGY AS A FORCE MULTIPLIER FOR GOOD, WE CANNOT STAY POLARIZED FROM EACH OTHER

THE TEN COMMANDMENTS OF WORK RELATIONSHIPS

As you undertake this journey into greater self-awareness, here are ways to improve interpersonal relationships— especially with bosses and coworkers. These tips are so important, we call them the "Ten Commandments of Work Relationships."

01 THOU SHALT DROP YOUR EGO

Ego is not your amigo. You can't think you have the power to "fix" other people—or that the world would be a far better place if you were in charge.

02 THOU SHALT HIT THE PAUSE BUTTON

When you're triggered by something your boss or a coworker says or does, you can't react like a sprinter off the blocks. Pause between the stimulus and your reaction. Speak too fast and you'll regret it later. The old "counting to 10" maneuver can

prevent you from saying or doing anything that
only escalates the conflict. And that pause should
be doubled if you're furiously thumbing an email
or text to respond to something someone just said.

03 THOU SHALT REMEMBER THE GOLDEN RULE

Treat others the way you want to be treated. When in
doubt, rely on empathy, authenticity, and compassion.
When you can show a little humility and remember
your humanity (saying "good morning" or "thank you"),
you'll be surprised how much negativity can be defused.

> ## WHEN IN DOUBT, RELY ON EMPATHY, AUTHENTICITY, AND COMPASSION

04 THOU SHALT MAKE OTHERS FEEL BETTER AFTER EVERY INTERACTION

Early in my career, someone gave me some amazing
advice. People should always feel better after
they've spoken with you—even if it's a difficult

conversation—or even a text or WeChat. How? By focusing on the issues that need to be acknowledged and the problems that can't be ignored. Ask for and listen to the opinions of others.

05 THOU SHALT SEEK TO UNDERSTAND OTHERS BEFORE BEING UNDERSTOOD

Among Dr. Stephen Covey's 7 Habits of Highly Effective People, one of my favorites is "seek first to understand, then be understood." What makes others tick? What's important to them? What's their communication style? What are their strengths and weaknesses? View your coworkers through the lens of seeking to understand— instead of trying to make yourself understood.

06 THOU SHALT LISTEN TWICE AS MUCH AS YOU SPEAK

We all have two ears and one mouth for a reason— listening twice as much as we speak. Listen to understand and take in information. Listen without interrupting—not waiting for the other person to take a breath so you can jump in. Don't rush to judge; ask questions if you don't understand.

07 THOU SHALT BE OPEN TO FEEDBACK

Are you part of the problem—or part of the solution? In almost any workplace conflict, you're on one side or the other. Maybe you didn't start it, but if you complain to any and all who will listen and play passive-aggressive games, you are escalating the problem. Do you say one thing but do another? These habits may be so ingrained, you may not even be aware of your own behaviors. Get feedback from a mentor or trusted advisor on how you might handle the challenge, especially if the conflict is with your manager.

> **GET FEEDBACK FROM A MENTOR OR TRUSTED ADVISOR ON HOW YOU MIGHT HANDLE THE CHALLENGE**

08 THOU SHALT CEASE THE GRIPE SESSIONS

A constant theme in workplace conversations is talking about the boss or complaining about a coworker. ("You're not going to believe what they said/

did today!") Stop! What does anyone get out of feeding the negativity? It only escalates stress for everyone. Unless there is a breach of ethics or integrity—in which case, this becomes a human resources issue—let it go and move on.

09 THOU SHALT ASSUME THE BETTER MOTIVE

Your boss gives you a last-minute assignment late on a Friday and needs it done by midday Monday. Your coworker announces there's a major problem, and suddenly you're dragged in to help solve it. This happens all the time in organizations. Priorities shift and things escalate. Maybe the boss just got handed that assignment from on high. Maybe your coworker just uncovered a problem while it's still contained, before it becomes an even bigger issue. When in doubt, assume the better motive. You have to do the work anyway, so you might as well put a better spin on it.

> YOU HAVE TO DO THE WORK ANYWAY, SO YOU MIGHT AS WELL PUT A BETTER SPIN ON IT

10

THOU SHALT
ASK FOR AND
OFFER HELP

Virtually everyone is good at something, and chances are your colleagues have strengths that you lack and vice versa. As you work together on a joint project or team initiative, focus on what each person brings. The more clearly you can see your colleagues, the better you'll understand how to work with them. What help can you offer to get the job done? What help can you ask for? Working together, focused on a common problem, can help build bridges.

THE MORE CLEARLY YOU CAN SEE YOUR COLLEAGUES, THE BETTER YOU'LL UNDERSTAND HOW TO WORK WITH THEM

With commitment, greater awareness, and a willingness to change your own behavior, you can put these Ten Commandments to work every day.

PARTNERING WITH YOUR BOSS

G ood bosses are amazing role models who embody the behaviors they want to see in others. And there's nothing like working for a great boss who champions and mentors others, invests in their success and development, and gives their team members ample opportunities to learn and grow. But having a good manager only happens about one-third to half of the time—and great is a rare bird indeed.

Far more common, unfortunately, is having a bad boss. Some bosses are only mildly bad; but there can be far more challenging ones as well—hypercritical, unreliable, and sometimes outright duplicitous.

That's why people usually don't quit jobs—they quit bosses. In a strong job market, it may seem easy to say, "I'm outta here." But the truth is, bosses are temporary—either they'll move on, or you will. In the meantime, there are important skills to learn about managing—and even partnering with—your boss.

—

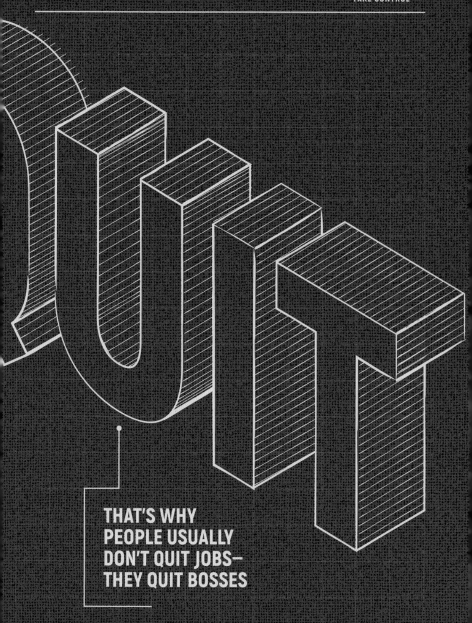

THAT'S WHY
PEOPLE USUALLY
DON'T QUIT JOBS—
THEY QUIT BOSSES

YOU CAN ONLY CHANGE YOURSELF

One of the biggest mistakes people make with bosses is trying to change them. That won't work. Actually, it's up to you—adjusting and shifting. After all, since you are the only one you can change, you need to address your own attitudes and behaviors.

NO MATTER WHAT THE PROBLEM TURNS OUT TO BE, YOU HOLD THE SOLUTION

The starting place is to pinpoint the problem and its cause. No matter what the problem turns out to be, you hold the solution. By becoming more self-aware of your attitudes, judgments, behaviors, and tendency to react negatively, you can defuse a lot of the tension. In fact, this is an opportunity for you to learn and grow as you control your emotions, manage your behaviors, and determine how best to respond.

The result will be less stress for you and a more manageable working relationship with your boss.

—

COMMUNICATING—CONTENT AND FREQUENCY

One of the key areas of your boss relationship is how you communicate—both the content and the frequency. Your manager may be one of those people who wants to know everything (a micromanager). Or maybe the exact opposite—your manager is too focused on everything and everyone else to get into the nitty-gritty with you.

When in doubt—ask. Find out what the boss wants to hear from you—how and how often. Once you know the expectations, then you can communicate accordingly.

But here's the thing: The bulk of your communication with your manager is going to be performance-related, so you need to make sure you are performing. When you're unhappy with someone, it's too easy to turn passive aggressive. Your manager wants something done today; you decide you'll get around to it—eventually. This will only perpetuate unhealthy conflict and, ultimately, become self-destructive.

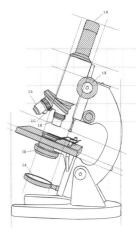

STAY FOCUSED ON WHAT NEEDS TO BE DONE, ESPECIALLY IN THE SHORT TERM

Stay focused on what needs to be done, especially in the short term. What project or task has the highest priority? What needs to be done right now? It's all about knowing the goals and priorities for your team or department and making them your priorities too.

And this benefits you, as well. By engaging with the work, you'll be more likely to rise above.

—

DON'T MAKE IT PERSONAL

It's time for a little perspective. Your boss has a lot more to think about than just you. There are simply too many people, projects, and priorities to be managed. That's why compartmentalization is a must-have skill for managers.

However, some managers—and especially those who are newly promoted into the role—have not yet mastered the art of compartmentalizing. As a result, they get caught up in their own projects—or they may be feeling frustrated about something else (personal or professional).

So, that lack of response to what you just said, or the feedback that sounded a little harsh, may very well have nothing to do with you. You've just encountered the moody trickle-down effect. Don't make it personal. Keep your focus on what needs to get done.

—

DON'T MAKE IT PERSONAL,

KEEP YOUR FOCUS ON WHAT NEEDS TO GET DONE

MANAGING THE MICROMANAGER

Micromanaging is one of the most common complaints about bosses. Micromanagers are known for their heavy scrutiny, constant texting and emailing to "check on things," and passive-aggressive comments. Micromanaging may be hardwired into the boss's personality.

Your game plan? Apply reverse micromanagement. If information is what makes your boss feel better (read: more in control), then provide more information before the boss asks for it. It can be as simple as sending an email with your plan for the day or week before your manager asks what you're working on. You can take it to the next step by sending an email at the end of the day or week to summarize what you've accomplished and what will come next. Over time, this flow of information builds trust, and your manager may loosen the reins a little bit.

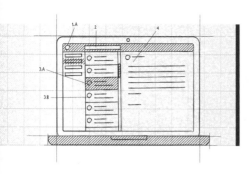

OVER TIME, THIS FLOW OF INFORMATION BUILDS TRUST, AND YOUR MANAGER MAY LOOSEN THE REINS A BIT

A little advice to the wise—pick your battles. There will be some things you should just let go. If you choose your battles, you may also become less emotional, which could make your manager more likely to listen and engage with you.

With the Micromanager, or any other difficult manager, you'll be able to gain control—gradually. Sometimes it's a gain of only inches, and it must be done artfully. As you establish rapport with your boss, you can introduce more trust into the relationship.

—

WHAT A BAD BOSS CAN TEACH YOU

If there is one positive outcome from working for a bad boss, this is it—the experience will teach you how not to treat others. It's true—people are much more likely to learn compassion and integrity from a bad boss than a good one. When you know firsthand how horrible it feels to be subjected to a bad boss's behavior (unless it crosses the line, in which case it must be reported), it's unlikely that you'd ever do that to someone else. So, while there's some short-term pain, the long-term gain is greater self-awareness and a deeper realization of the importance of valuing others.

CONNECTING WITH COWORKERS

From bosses, we move on to another workplace relationship: the one you have with your colleagues. Over the years, you'll have coworkers who feel like family. And there will be some you could probably do without.

Fortunately, there are coping strategies to help you manage your coworker relationships. But first you need to discern the problem—and then (just as you did with difficult bosses) adjust your behavior. Let's take one of the most common examples of a difficult coworker—the chronic complainer.

FIRST YOU NEED TO DISCERN THE PROBLEM

I learned this many years ago when I was working at a consulting firm. Seven of us were on a project together. We had different backgrounds and perspectives, which should have made us highly innovative. Except one of our teammates only saw the worst possible outcome in every scenario. This colleague shot down new ideas like a skeet shooter at target practice. *That will never work...We tried that before...It's just too risky...No one will go for it...How's that going to work with the budget we have?* This colleague wasn't intentionally trying to derail the team; rather, this person was just hardwired never to see the blue sky—only "the sky is falling." The problem was that, with this colleague on the team, even great ideas turned into bad ideas. We were all brought down—really down. In the end, the constant complaining was so emotionally taxing on the team, we were not successful.

When people are chronic complainers, they're draining energy.

—

CONSTRUCTIVE COMPLAINING— FROM BUT TO AND

There's one type of complaint that we should all welcome: those that bring issues out into the open. That's "constructive" complaining that is accompanied by an idea, a solution, or at least some additional insight.

It might sound oxymoronic: complaining that's actually constructive. But it's a great way to generate energy into finding solutions.

The fact is, there's nothing inherently wrong with complaints, the same way there's nothing wrong with conflict (as we'll discuss in a moment). Both can actually spark the creative process as people own the problem and brainstorm with each other. Over time, constructive complaining (along with creative conflict) can forge a culture in which people aren't afraid to speak the truth, take on issues, and find new ways forward. But it does take effort.

It starts with mutual understanding and respect. That means we need to stop rushing to judge others or dismiss their ideas and suggestions. People aren't wrong in their thoughts or approaches—they're simply different! For example, you may conclude that (in your view), your colleagues are wasting time ruminating while you're typically fast to act. These differences aren't a problem unless you make it so. Differences strengthen the team. Your colleagues' ability to see all sides of a problem or situation is a definite plus, especially when combined with your fast decision-making.

—

ENERGIZING TEAM DISCUSSIONS

Nothing shoots down a group discussion faster than "but." One person floats an idea, and another person jumps in with "but" (or similar negative words and nonverbals). That's an interesting idea but the problem is ... what comes next is always negative, and it invariably leads to disagreement. To improve team effectiveness, replace "but" with "and." That's an interesting idea, and you might also consider X. You can actually feel the energy in the room start to rise.

WE'RE ALL IN
THIS TOGETHER

What brings people together is a sense of shared
purpose to accomplish a common mission, an
overarching goal.

I saw this among my own children several years ago,
while on vacation. On our last day, as all seven of us
scrambled to pack and get to the airport on time, in our
rush somebody knocked over a fruit smoothie and sent
it flying. Standing at the door, luggage in each hand,
I watched as that pink lava, as if in slow motion, shot
into the air and landed with a splat—right on a white
rug, of course.

We all sprang into action. It was orchestrated chaos, and
everyone had a role. Someone grabbed bath towels to
sop up the mess. Someone else squirted shampoo (the
only "cleaner" we had) to avoid a stain. Another person
doused it with water. After a lot of rubbing and scrubbing,
somebody pulled out the hairdryer—and nearly burned
the rug. We felt like the Keystone Kops.

But out of uncertainty and chaos, things get done. It's
the same for all of us today: when we come together as
a team, we can work together—and turn our individual
activities into real accomplishment.

RED LIGHT, GREEN LIGHT

S ome people will rub you the wrong way because of their personality. Their style is different from yours—formal to your casual (or vice versa). Or maybe they have a habit that irks you. They talk too much—like that "let me tell you about my crazy weekend" person who can't wait to speak with you first thing on Monday morning. Or they talk too little—sharing next to nothing with coworkers.

BEHAVIORS, HOWEVER, ARE AN ENTIRELY DIFFERENT MATTER. THEY'RE ALL ABOUT HOW PEOPLE TREAT AND INTERACT WITH OTHERS

Behaviors, however, are an entirely different matter. They're all about how people treat and interact with others. Basically, behaviors fall into three categories. To illustrate, I'll use the analogy of a stoplight:

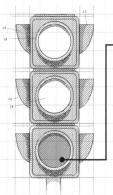

GREEN LIGHT:

Everyone is in sync and gets along. People enjoy collaborating. They're positive and encouraging of one another. It's rare—but if you find it, then it's a green light all the way!

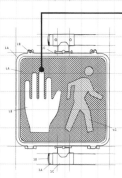

RED LIGHT:

If you encounter harassing or bullying behaviors, or if you feel unsafe or threatened in any way by a coworker, then you must escalate the matter immediately to your boss and to human resources. This is an intolerable situation and must be stopped.

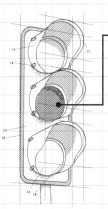

YELLOW LIGHT:

The far larger and more common category is in between, with an array of behaviors and interactions that are problematic. Some you can shrug off, others must be addressed. Deciding how to address them is where the flashing caution light comes in. You need to discern how best to respond.

—

COLLECTIVE GENIUS

I t's been said that the strength of a team is each individual member—and the strength of each member is the team. To experience this, we must buy into the concept of "collective genius."

Research shows that, in the early stages, teams that are composed of people who are all alike (homogeneous) outperform those that are diverse. The reason is a lack of disruption and conflict that can result when different perspectives, experiences, backgrounds, thinking, and communication styles are merged. However, over time, well-managed diverse teams significantly outperform well-managed homogeneous teams.

WHEN TEAMS MOVE FROM DIVERSITY TO INCLUSION— WHERE DIFFERENCES ARE NOT JUST TOLERATED BUT ALSO CELEBRATED—

When teams move from diversity to inclusion—where differences are not just tolerated but also celebrated— they show greater innovation and strategic thinking. That's how we can leverage our differences into collective genius.

—

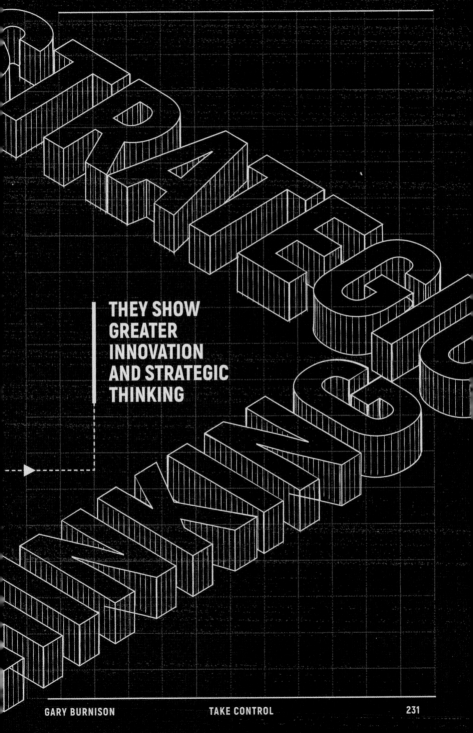

THEY SHOW
GREATER
INNOVATION
AND STRATEGIC
THINKING

DEALING WITH STRESS—IT'S DIFFERENT FOR EVERYBODY

As business accelerates with faster, more frequent deadlines, stress also accelerates. Not everybody reacts to the same stresses. Among your coworkers, you may find people who "lose it" as soon as there is a hint of pressure, while others never seem to break a sweat. Instead of judging your coworkers' reactions to stress, understand that their reactions are just different than yours.

Daniel Goleman, in his extensive research and writing about emotional intelligence, advises that people are more likely to keep an open mind (and an even keel) if they get better at their own stress management. Here are some tips that may help:

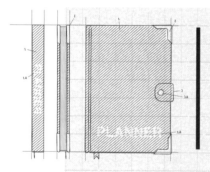

AS BUSINESS ACCELERATES WITH FASTER, MORE FREQUENT DEADLINES, STRESS ALSO ACCELERATES

- Go for a 10-minute walk.

- Reflect on the root cause of your stress.

- Consider alternative solutions or paths.

- Contextualize the moment in the whole of your life.

- Call or text a friend you haven't spoken to in a while.

- Look at pictures of your loved ones.

- Immerse yourself in your favorite music, comedians, or online videos.

These simple steps can help you improve self-management and achieve "emotional balance"—improving your ability to handle anxiety, anger, and frustration. You may even find that, as your stress levels decrease, your workplace relationships can really improve.

—

TAKE CONTROL

Chapter 9

NAVIGATING YOUR COMPANY'S CULTURE TO GET AHEAD

If we think about it, companies are a lot like families. There are spoken and unspoken rules about what's acceptable and what's not. For instance, is it OK to eat dinner in the living room, feet up on the coffee table? Or are meals only to be eaten at the kitchen table? If you're new to the family and don't know the culture, you could end up doing the wrong thing or, worse yet, offending someone.

When I was growing up, the minute I walked into my aunt's house, I had to kick off my sneakers at the door. The reason? The pride of this Midwest household was a white shag carpet, and my aunt kept it spotless. There were clear plastic runners across the rug to walk on, which matched the plastic coverings on the furniture. Best of all—they raked the carpet with this special rake to make it look like new.

I didn't have to do any of these things at home—but their house, their rules. When I got a little older, though, it occurred to me why these things were so important. My aunt and uncle didn't have a lot of money, and they worked hard for anything they had—she as a nurse, and he at an oil refinery.

Their rules communicated their work ethic and values. That was the culture that made their house a home.

Organizations are no different—they have their own "house rules." For some, it's okay to work anywhere, anytime. Others want to go back to the days of everyone in the office. Many are somewhere in between.

ORGANIZATIONS ARE NO DIFFERENT—THEY HAVE THEIR OWN "HOUSE RULES"

But just like the carpet rake and the plastic runners, that's all just the form—the protocols and procedures. Far more important is the substance—how people actually engage and interact with each other. That's the essence of culture.

—

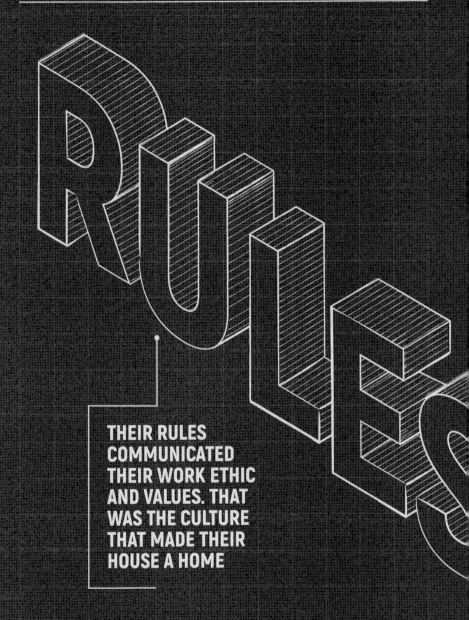

THEIR RULES
COMMUNICATED
THEIR WORK ETHIC
AND VALUES. THAT
WAS THE CULTURE
THAT MADE THEIR
HOUSE A HOME

THE CULTURE CONUNDRUM

Ask six people to define culture, and you'll probably get twelve different answers. Some will say it's the mission and values. For others it's about work attire and where you work.

Culture, though, boils down to just one definition—it's how things get done.

You won't find it spelled out in some handbook. It's not captured in some slogan on a website or a poster in the hallway. Culture needs to be experienced to be understood.

Easy to visualize, but difficult to actualize—that's culture. I can remember a client meeting a few years ago, when every member of their senior team was asked to define their culture. As each person spoke, it became clear that they were focused only on the form—not the substance. But when the question changed—"What is it like to be an employee here?"—the answers were from the heart, stripped of jargon, and laser focused on how work gets done.

The fact is everyone is trying to figure out the workplace these days. But too often the focus is all about the *where* and not enough about the *why*. Defining culture is far more than just deciding on office space and real estate.

And culture certainly isn't about the company logo on a shirt or taking your dog to work—what the experts call the artifacts of culture. What matters most is what's behind those artifacts—the beliefs, behaviors, and shared mindset that are at the heart of a collective culture.

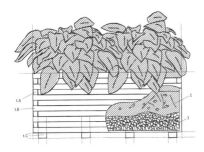

FOR EMPLOYEES, IT'S ABOUT COMMUNITY AND OPPORTUNITY— HOW THEY CAN BE PART OF SOMETHING BIGGER THAN THEMSELVES

For employees, it's about community and opportunity— how they can be part of something bigger than themselves and receive the coaching, mentoring, and sponsorship they need to advance. For organizations, it's about connection, commitment, and culture that have the biggest influence on how things get done.

—

BUILDING YOUR POLITICAL CAPITAL

Learning to navigate culture has another important payoff: It's essential for developing what's known as "political capital." The truth is, we can't advance in our careers—let alone take control of them—if we don't build political capital. You can't just acquire it—you need to earn it through relationships with others, especially those above you. Once you have political capital, you can more easily create buy-in and get things done.

The goal is to become as politically savvy as you can within your organization. Now, don't confuse this with being "political"—a term often used as code for not always being trusted by others. Rather, by being politically savvy, you can influence those around you—and even above you.

—

WHAT DETERMINES YOUR POLITICAL CAPITAL?

Political capital is like any other kind of capital. It must be accrued over time. It's depleted the more you spend it, and you have to replenish it regularly.

The amount of political capital you have depends largely on one crucial factor: the amount of trust others have in you. Trust comes down to keeping your word. Watch your say/do ratio. If it isn't 1:1—you say what you mean and do what you say—your political capital won't grow. And when you need to build capital quickly, doing what you say you will do (and frequently exceeding expectations) is crucial.

Trust can also come through bonding. You were part of a team that handled a difficult project or even a crisis. You were really in the trenches together. You may even bond over common interests—for example, you both volunteered for or participated in a fund-raiser for a cause that's personal and important to both of you. It goes without saying: Your passion for the cause must be authentic.

Most important, you need to be inclusive—by your words and actions showing that you appreciate and value every person and their unique differences. And, if you aspire to greater influence within your organization, being anything but an inclusive leader would be oxymoronic. True leadership is inherently inclusive: leading the many while at the same time understanding the perspectives of each.

TRUE LEADERSHIP IS INHERENTLY INCLUSIVE: LEADING THE MANY WHILE AT THE SAME TIME UNDERSTANDING THE PERSPECTIVES OF EACH

When an inclusive environment truly exists, people know it's safe to be themselves and speak their truth. They freely share observations and perspectives. Feedback should bubble up from within the organization, instead of merely cascading down. Helping to make your organization more inclusive is a powerful way to build political capital—for the good of all.

So, how do you do that? The short answer is it depends. Every organization is different and so are the nuances of building political capital. But there are some basic ground rules.

For example, you may work for a company that prides itself on having few titles and even fewer layers. Good ideas can come from anywhere, and every voice gets to be heard. But even in a flat organization, which appears to be so nonhierarchical, you need to understand who has influence and who doesn't. Who can expedite or stonewall things?

If you're new to a company or you've joined a new team, this will take some figuring out. Even if you've been around for a few years, things may have shifted because of other changes, such as a new boss or boss's boss. Promotions, transfers, teams expanding or contracting— all of it changes the dynamics.

BUILDING YOUR POLITICAL CAPITAL IS A PROCESS—JUST LIKE ANY OTHER

Building your political capital is a process—just like any other. It takes time and attention.

—

SPENDING YOUR CAPITAL

When you have amassed political capital, you can spend it to further your goals, such as getting help to land that assignment you want or an introduction to someone higher up in the organization, or even assistance in tackling a problem that's bigger than you realized.

But don't overestimate the amount of political capital you have. Reciprocity is a real thing: You need to give to get, always being consistent in your performance and showing high integrity in your actions.

WHEN YOU HAVE AMASSED POLITICAL CAPITAL, YOU CAN SPEND IT TO FURTHER YOUR GOALS

NAVIGATING THE NETWORKS

Now that you understand the ground rules of building political capital, let's take it a step deeper. What does this look like in action?

Organizations are complex mazes of personalities, constituencies, issues, and rivalries. There are people with strong egos and those who are looking to amass their own power. And everything in between.

ORGANIZATIONS ARE COMPLEX MAZES OF PERSONALITIES, CONSTITUENCIES, ISSUES, AND RIVALRIES

Forget the organizational chart. There are informal networks and unwritten rules about how things get done and by whom. You need to figure out who really has "the juice." The easiest way is to see who can spend the money. Who can hire and fire? And then there are those who have the power behind the scenes; they may not be as obvious at first—and it shifts!

Think about the big boss's assistant, who controls both the calendar and the access. And then there's the person who operates way behind the scenes—nobody even knows his or her exact title or responsibilities. But this person's name is mentioned with a tone that's somewhere between awe and fear.

Swirling around are the power grabbers and the political operators. They're the ones who are trying to seize visibility and power. This doesn't happen everywhere to the same degree. But people being people—just as in a big extended family full of personalities and history—there will be cliques and alliances.

Given all that, someone might be tempted to just stay out of the whole mess. But that won't serve you, either. Rather, you need to discern the networks and nuances—from your boss to your boss's boss to the "influencers." In other words, you need to keep your eyes and ears open to the web of relationships that are also part of how things get done.

—

YOUR EI: DON'T GO ANYWHERE WITHOUT IT

To be politically savvy; you need an all-important skill that will serve you well throughout your career: emotional intelligence (EI). As we've discussed already, you need EI for many reasons related to your advancement—from getting along with your boss, to managing and motivating others, to relating to people across cultures and context. In this discussion of discerning and navigating office politics, you can't survive without EI.

EI is composed of empathy, adaptability, self-awareness, and similar competencies. Research suggests that EI is twice as important as cognitive ability (better known as IQ) in predicting performance. Given just how potent EI is in the workplace, it's clear you need to develop it, particularly when navigating office politics.

RESEARCH SUGGESTS THAT EI IS TWICE AS IMPORTANT AS COGNITIVE ABILITY

Here are a few EI tips to raise your profile and help build your political savvy:

• WHO'S ON FIRST?

Whether you're in a room or on a Zoom, notice where the power is—and don't assume it's with the boss. It may be a star performer or a group of people who are closely aligned with the boss. Where are the alliances and where are the factions? This will tell you whose ideas are more likely to garner support—and whose support you'll need for your own ideas. Also, be on the lookout for those who always seem to know what's going on and whom others go to for advice. These are the tracings of the networks that exist within teams, departments, and companies. You'll want to know where they are, who's on them, and how you can

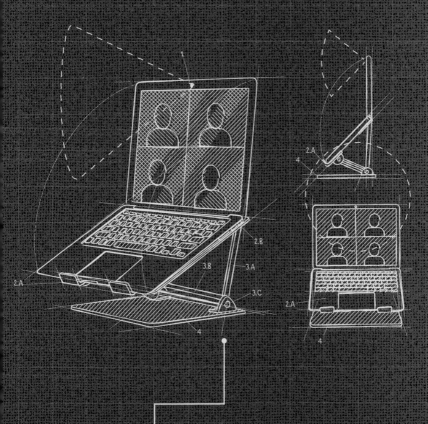

WHETHER YOU'RE
IN A ROOM OR ON A
ZOOM, NOTICE WHERE
THE POWER IS—AND
DON'T ASSUME IT'S
WITH THE BOSS

join. You need to align yourself with the decision-makers and influencers who can put a word in for you on that bigger assignment. And when there's a task force or cross-department initiative, they'll want you to be part of the team. You can't push it, but the higher your performance, the more you'll get noticed.

THE CONTAGION FACTOR

Team members, particularly leaders, can transmit their feelings, positive or negative, to others. With emotional self-awareness, you can ensure that you're sending more positive feelings than negative ones—and that can help make a big improvement in the team dynamic. A can-do attitude may be cliché, but it works. Let's say you know the next team meeting or project update is bound to result in a debate. How might your colleagues react? What are your own feelings? How can you engage in the discussion in a way that turns opposing views into constructive conflict that yields meaningful discussion?

BE "PEOPLE SENSITIVE"

Learning to read people is a great skill, and it will serve you well in your career. You'll need your best observation skills. How do people react to stress, challenges, opportunities, and failure?

See beyond the behaviors to the motivation that's driving those behaviors. How do people act in meetings? What are formal and informal conversations like? The more you can read the people around you, the better you can adjust your approach to influence others.

· A WORD OF CAUTION

Building trust and accumulating political capital takes time and trust. But all that can be destroyed quickly by missteps and poor choices. If you are told something in confidence, keep it that way. If you must discuss something, don't associate names with it.

—

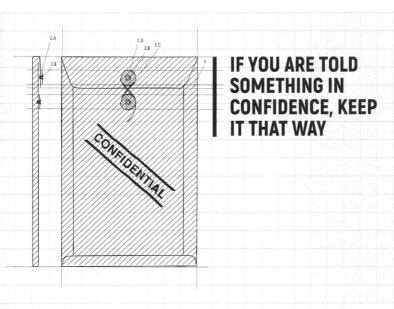

IF YOU ARE TOLD SOMETHING IN CONFIDENCE, KEEP IT THAT WAY

THE MOST INFLUENTIAL PEOPLE YOU NEVER WANT TO SNUB

Guess who? Where your mind goes first is a window into your political savvy. If you immediately went to senior leadership, you're thinking hierarchically—bigger title, more influence. But that's too obvious.

Ken Blanchard, the acclaimed management expert, shared a story with me about a pilot who was applying for a job at another airline. Now, this was a very experienced pilot with the kind of skills any airline would be glad to have. But on the flight to where the airline was based the pilot was rude to the crew. At corporate headquarters, the pilot was dismissive of not one but two people who greeted him. One of those employees called HR and reported everything, including the tip-off from the flight crew about the pilot's bad behavior. The upshot? The pilot was sent home without ever getting the interview.

So now who do you think are the most influential people you never want to snub? If you said everyone and anyone, you got that right. Never assume that someone with a seemingly unimpressive title doesn't have influence and access. There are people behind the scenes whom senior leaders rely on for everything from institutional knowledge to accomplishing the seemingly impossible. These are the people you need to identify and align yourself with.

—

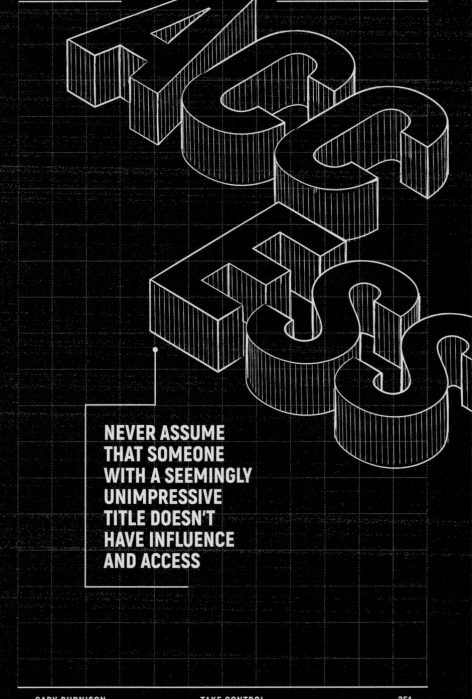

NEVER ASSUME
THAT SOMEONE
WITH A SEEMINGLY
UNIMPRESSIVE
TITLE DOESN'T
HAVE INFLUENCE
AND ACCESS

GETTING "BUY-IN"

Now that you've built all this political capital, especially with your boss, you don't want to diminish it—or worse yet, lose it— because of an unwise move. But that doesn't mean you should play it too safe, either.

Taking no risks is a real risk and may single you out as someone who can't take on a bigger job or broader responsibilities. Most companies today encourage risk-taking, creativity, and pushing boundaries. Even failure is embraced—as long as failure happens fast and the learning happens even faster. (Psychologists refer to this as having "psychological safety"— meaning you won't be punished if you make a mistake.)

But unless you're among the rare disrupters—Elon Musk or the late Steve Jobs, who rocked their companies and their industries—you need to figure out how to do this. For 99 percent of us, it will mean getting buy-in, starting with your boss.

Tune into your emotional intelligence. How does your company react to the new and different? Consider what happened to the last person who tried a new idea that didn't work out. Is that person still there? How did the organization respond? Were more resources brought in to help problem-solve and strategize? Or did people run for the corners while waiting to see who was thrown under the bus?

Once you understand how your organization handles risk-taking, you can decide how to present new ideas or try to change "how we've always done things." Rather than jumping into the deep end with no life preserver, it's probably more politically astute to wade in. Test the waters, see if you're likely to sink or swim, and then go in a little deeper. Here are some tips for how to make that happen:

· FLOAT THE IDEA

Let's say you've got an idea for a new approach, a better way of doing things, or another way to attack the problem. It may be an innovation. Or you may be trying to overhaul how things have always been done. These are all political moves because they test conventional wisdom and depart from the tried-and-true. People are usually averse to change, which means it's better to start by floating the idea, especially with your boss. Your objective is to start the conversation and plant the idea in your manager's head. If you get the green light, then off you go! But what if the response is lukewarm at best or an outright rejection? If your boss has the final say on everything, then hearing no at the outset probably killed your idea (at least for now). If you keep pushing it, you won't get anywhere and could end up hurting yourself.

• WADE IN DEEPER

If you get or feel some leeway, you may be able to keep the idea alive. When there is a chance to maneuver, take a step into deeper water. You need evidence—that means research and real data—to back up your plan. If you go to your boss with real facts, you're more likely to get buy-in, and your boss is more likely to support you.

• GET YOUR PEERS ON BOARD

Here's where positive peer pressure really works. One person makes (or pushes for) a positive change and then others start to join in. The more people who get behind this new idea or approach, the more likely others will come along.

• TAKE THE PLUNGE

This won't happen often, but there may be times when you go all in—committing yourself to pushing ahead no matter what—especially if enough of your peers are with you. If your manager is known for giving the team a fair amount of autonomy, then that may be the green light you need to proceed.

Taking control of the career you want, where you want, is not simply titles, promotions, pay, and locations. To take control, you need to navigate the culture, which will vary from company to company and the people who work there.

—

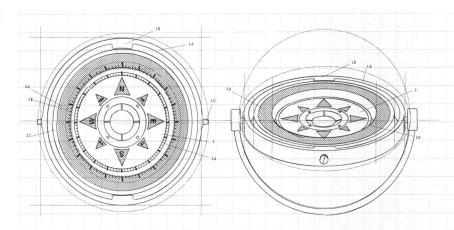

TO TAKE CONTROL, YOU NEED TO NAVIGATE THE CULTURE, WHICH WILL VARY FROM COMPANY TO COMPANY AND THE PEOPLE WHO WORK THERE.

Chapter 10

COMMUNICATING AND CONNECTING

If there is one last piece of advice I can offer for your career, this is it: You are your message. It applies at every stage, and especially as you become a manager and, perhaps, move up into a leadership role. Along the way, your communication skills—oral, written, and digital—are crucial to your career development. Become known as a good communicator, and you'll be given more opportunities—including to lead others.

You don't have to become a great orator. But you do need to communicate clearly, concisely, and in a way that engages and motivates others.

Communication is the true "information highway"— critical for building alignment and executing strategy. And it flows in both directions. Communication is important in good times and imperative in challenging ones.

Depending on where you are in your career, much of your communication is probably with your boss (and we all have them). A good rule of thumb is, when in doubt, overcommunicate. Most of that communication will be about the most pressing projects and priorities. Not only will that eliminate any question as to what you're working on, but you will also be able to convey in real time what challenges you're encountering.

A GOOD RULE OF THUMB IS, WHEN IN DOUBT, OVERCOMMUNICATE

There is nothing more frustrating for any manager or leader, and at any level, than when people keep saying, "Everything's fine—no problems here," only to find out later that there really was a problem. If someone had only spoken up sooner, that problem could have been addressed when it was smaller, instead of allowing it to snowball into something more complex and difficult to solve.

As the saying goes—speak truth to power. A good boss will appreciate it, and you'll gain a reputation for being truthful and trustworthy.

The same principle applies when you're communicating with the team you're leading, whether 5 people, 50,

500, 5,000 or 50,000. Over the years, and in leading others through crisis—from the Great Recession to the pandemic—I've come to appreciate how much people would rather know the truth than dwell in the worst-case scenarios residing in their imaginations. If not addressed, a lack of information can lead to hazardous uncertainty.

If knowledge is power, then people need to be empowered by information. Otherwise, they'll spend their time speculating because there's an information vacuum that needs to be filled. Uncertainty breeds conjecture, escalating fear and causing chaos. No matter how serious the news, people want the truth—delivered with facts and hope.

—

ACTIONS SPEAK LOUDER

Over time, and as your career develops, you'll probably discover a truth as I did over the years: Communication is where leadership lives and breathes.

In short, language is an art to express ideas—but the messenger is the message. "Actions speak louder than words" is true for everyone—and twice as true for those who lead others. Verbally and nonverbally, the way in which communication occurs—humbly, passionately, confidently—has more impact than merely the words chosen.

—

WE-DERSHIP NOT ME-DERSHIP

The only time for "I" is when taking accountability—such as making tough decisions and being willing to accept the consequences for them. As you move up in your career, you'll see that there is no room for egocentric "me-dership." Your job will be to encourage followership through "we-dership" that focuses on a common purpose and shared goals. It really is about "we."

THE ONLY TIME FOR "I" IS WHEN TAKING ACCOUNTABILITY

YOU'RE NEVER *NOT* COMMUNICATING

When I first became a CEO, some 15 years ago, I did not fully grasp a pervasive reality: The leader is never not communicating. In those early days, I was so focused on the "message moments" and their content— bold speeches and judiciously worded memos—that I failed to notice that I was still "broadcasting" the rest of the time, and with the rest of my body.

That meant everything I said and did not say, the words I chose or avoided, where my eyes focused, the relative ease and speed of my gait when I moved, whether I used this story or that one, whether my voice was calm or commanding .... All of that contained tiny messages that others picked up on, consciously and unconsciously.

To be a more effective communicator, I needed to recognize the importance of each of those moments and master them. Of course, content matters. There is no room for offhand, ill-considered remarks. People will take you literally, so be clear, precise, and constantly aware of the impact of your words.

If all that sounds like a tall order, relax. Just as with every skill, you'll develop it over time and with experience. Along the way, though, you'll need to be aware of the pitfalls. Avoid these mistakes, and you'll propel yourself along the communication learning curve.

—

10 DIGITAL DEADLY SINS

Ironically, perhaps, one of the biggest pitfalls is digital communication. The very mode of communication that keeps us connected—anytime, anywhere—can also cause friction and even fractures.

Digital communication is like breathing—it's second nature and we can't survive without it. The sheer volume and frequency of emails and texts make it easy to fire off a note or reply without thinking. That haste, though, is when some of the biggest and deadliest sins of digital communication can be sent. Here's what you should be aware of.

• THAT "PRIVATE" EMAIL JUST GOT FORWARDED

You assumed the email you wrote to one person—badmouthing the boss, making fun of colleagues, complaining about other departments—was never going to be seen by anyone else. But there it is, circulating around the department, and now your boss wants to talk to you. Always remember: Anyone can forward anything—and that includes texts too!

· YOUR "OK" JUST GOT SOMEONE MAD

So much of communication isn't what you say but how you say it, and that's the problem with digital: emails and texts have no context. You don't have a tone of voice, as with phone conversations. You don't have verbal and nonverbal cues, as when you're in person. Emails and texts land flat. Take the response "OK," for example. Is that begrudging? Agreeable? Enthusiastic? Can't tell—and someone's assumption may not match your intention.

SO MUCH OF COMMUNICATION ISN'T WHAT YOU SAY BUT HOW YOU SAY IT, AND THAT'S THE PROBLEM WITH DIGITAL

· YOUR  IS GETTING RIDICULOUS

I'm always amazed by how many emails and texts I receive, including in business, which are populated with emoji. I once received a message with a bizarre expression that had me puzzled. Was that a smile, a frown, or a gas bubble? I don't know, you tell me:

Don't overuse these little faces—and don't expect them to speak for you.

COMMUNICATING AND CONNECTING

• YOU GOT YOUR BOBS MIXED UP

There's Bob, your friend. And then there's Bob, your boss's boss. In your haste, you didn't double-check the auto-filled email address before hitting send. Then a sick feeling came over you. In your sent emails, you've written a gripe manifesto with (count 'em) three expletives, and it's sitting in the wrong Bob's email inbox.

• YOU SENT AN EMAIL IN ANGER

Never, ever a good idea. The more riled up you are, the more time you need to respond. One way is to write it all out in an email without any address on it and then delete it! Now that you have it out of your system, write a second email. Save it to drafts. Reread it a few times and then—if you're sure it isn't going to backfire on you—hit send.

• YOU DIDN'T PROOFRE@D YOUR EMAIL

The occasional typo is one thing, but multiple misspellings, obvious grammatical mistakes, and dropped words make you look sloppy (or worse). It's also a sign of disrespect to the recipient(s). Having a tagline that reads "Siri didn't proofread this for me" isn't an excuse! Read it back to yourself, preferably aloud.

• YOU CC THE ENTIRE ORG CHART

Does everyone really have to be on that email?
Transparency is one thing, but too many ccs
makes you look either naive or overly self-
promotional. Be discreet about the number
of people you cc and bcc on your emails.

TRANSPARENCY IS ONE THING, BUT TOO MANY CCS MAKES YOU LOOK EITHER NAIVE OR OVERLY SELF-PROMOTIONAL

• YOU REPLY ALL, ALL THE TIME

If there's one thing that will get on people's nerves,
it's the meaningless reply all that's sent to 17
people, 17 times. Unless absolutely necessary,
just reply—but not to all.

• YOU THINK RECALLING YOUR MESSAGE ERASES IT FROM MEMORY

It rarely works. And human nature being what it
is, when people receive a recall on an email, they
can't wait to find the original and see what the
issue was.

- ## YOU TRY TO SOLVE THE PROBLEMS OF THE WORLD IN AN EMAIL

Just because you have as much space as you want to write in that email, don't. Digital communication should be concise. If you have that much to say, pick up the phone.

—

THE UNEXPECTED PERFORMANCE SKILL

As we move along the communication learning curve, presentation skills are often overlooked—but surprisingly impactful. We're not just talking about giving speeches in front of a crowded room, which few people do—especially these days. But the fact is, we always have opportunities to present— whether on the next team Zoom, in a formal client meeting, or more commonly on the impromptu call when your manager (or your manager's boss) asks for an update. Those who think on their feet and speak with poise and personality will often find themselves farther along on the path to promotion.

Unfortunately, when you say, "public speaking," most people freeze up. It ranks right up there with fear of death. (Comedian Jerry Seinfeld said it best: The person in the casket might be better off than the one giving the eulogy.) The problem is that most people are so focused on how they will be perceived and whether they'll be liked that they don't pay enough attention to others and what they need to hear.

Here are some tips that can help make you more polished and confident:

· WHO'S LISTENING?

This is the first question to consider when you're asked to make any presentation, big or small, formal or informal. To whom am I speaking and what do they want to know? It's all about them—so that, at the end, when they Zoom out or walk away they have exactly what they need.

· KNOW YOUR MESSAGE

You aren't downloading everything you can say on a topic; rather, you're targeting your message for others in that moment. Make an outline: three main points (more than that, and it becomes overload). Within each of those points, have three supporting points. Think sound bites—conveying your message 30 or 40 seconds at a time.

· LOSE THE POWERPOINT

Over the past several years, presentation prep has become increasingly focused on constructing good PowerPoint slides and far less on the words. But it's not a PowerPoint presentation. The presentation is done by a person—the slides are only the visuals, and the fewer the better. Don't expect people to read what's on the screen, whether you're sharing a document virtually or projecting it in front of an audience. If you must give detailed information, send a meeting brief in advance.

· PRACTICE, PRACTICE, PRACTICE

The more you practice, the more ingrained your message will become. Whether you're speaking to yourself in a mirror or to a friend in the room (or on a screen), practice conveying your key points and subpoints in the most concise, meaningful, and engaging way possible. Watch your body language. When you're in person, face the audience, keep your posture relaxed and confident, and use open and inviting hand gestures. Stay within the allotted time, with room for questions. And after every important interaction, take the time to reflect on how you can do even better next time.

—

TIPS FOR THE NEXT TIME YOU SPEAK ...

The team meeting. A conference call. Even a conversation in a hallway. Each is an opportunity to convey your ideas and yourself:

- It's not only what you say, but also how you say it—body language, facial expression, and nonverbal cues.

- Focus on your listeners—first, last, and always.

- Know what you are talking about— and be authentic and truthful about your expertise.

- Listen more than you talk—you want dialogue, not pontification.

- Keep to the point and respect people's time.

BRINGING OTHERS IN

Among your developed communication skills, you'll need to learn how to "break the ice" skillfully. This means engaging people in conversation—usually first about themselves, before moving on to your agenda. For example, I started a virtual meeting of about 10 people from around the globe by asking each person to say one interesting thing about themselves. As a result of this momentary sharing, we had one of the best meetings ever because people felt more personally and genuinely connected with the others.

AMONG YOUR DEVELOPED COMMUNICATION SKILLS, YOU'LL NEED TO LEARN HOW TO "BREAK THE ICE"

When it comes to icebreakers, I will admit that, in the past, I called "How are you?" the three most useless words in the world of communication. That's because this question is usually just filler—what people say when they don't know what else to say. Someone asks: "How are you?" and the automatic response is, "Fine, thanks. And you?"

But not anymore.

A silver lining to the upheaval of the last few years has been greater emotional intelligence, as people reach out personally, authentically, and frequently. Every conference call or conversation has started with sincere inquiries about how people and their loved ones were doing. As we move toward the "next normal," I don't see this changing.

Always and everywhere, these are the stories behind the stories that need to be shared

—

WHERE HEARING MEETS LISTENING

"Yep, yep, yep ..." Whenever we hear that response to something we're saying, we know the other person is only hearing—and not listening. It's code for "just get on with it" (as anyone with teenagers—or who has ever been a teenager—will tell you).

When someone is truly listening, they're paying close attention not only to the words, but more importantly to the silence—the pauses between the words—and the tone and emotion.

No doubt, we all know what the opposite feels like. For me, it happened a few years ago. My family and I were up

COMMUNICATING AND CONNECTING

half the night with Maddie, our beloved dog. Finally, at 3:36 a.m., we had to put Maddie down. The whole family was heartbroken.

A few hours later, with hardly any sleep, I headed into the office. I knew my energy level was low. So, when a client called me and asked, "How are you?" I took the question at face value and explained what had happened that night.

The reply? "Huh—" And then this person just continued with what they had to say.

I was stunned. I don't want to assume that this person didn't care. But clearly, they didn't care to listen.

And that's what we all must avoid. Listening is a long-term investment—when we give others our full and undivided attention. Indeed, listening is to hearing as observing is to seeing. Listening and observing are participative—we're all in and fully present.

LISTENING IS TO HEARING AS OBSERVING IS TO SEEING

When we truly listen, we let others know that they really do matter. We're interested not only in what they have to say, but also in who they are.

—

THE POWER OF STORIES

The best way to ensure that others are tuned into you and your message is to emotionalize and personalize your communication. And that's best done with stories. Just as the shamans of old gathered people around the fire to share wisdom and lore, you can also tap the power of storytelling.

After all, communication is not just transmitting information. It is also connecting emotionally with others to inspire them.

—

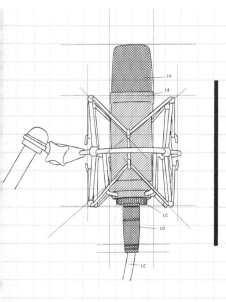

COMMUNICATION IS NOT JUST TRANSMITTING INFORMATION. IT IS ALSO CONNECTING EMOTIONALLY WITH OTHERS TO INSPIRE THEM

A SEA OF BUTTERFLIES

The message I wanted to convey was how, out of devastation, hope and rebirth emerge. My challenge was how to say that so that people didn't just hear the words; they actually felt them. Instantly, a story came to mind, about the wildfires a few years ago in California that destroyed millions of acres and countless homes and cost many lives.

> **MY CHALLENGE WAS HOW TO SAY THAT SO THAT PEOPLE DIDN'T JUST HEAR THE WORDS, THEY ACTUALLY FELT THEM**

The wildfire was perilously close to where I live, impacting thousands of people. Very late one night, as the air was thick with smoke and flames were visible in the hills nearby, I tied a bandana over my face and went outside to hose down our house. It was such a stupid, futile thing to do, but I couldn't just sit there and wait. I had to pretend I was in control.

At around midnight, my wife yelled to me, "We're out of here!" She preceded the fire department's evacuation by seconds. Minutes later we left, taking with us only photographs of our kids when they were younger; these were memories that could never be replaced.

Many houses in our neighborhood burned to the ground, though several (including ours) were spared by a shift in the wind. That night we experienced pure powerlessness against a wave of devastation that had come out of nowhere and mushroomed into a life-threatening risk. It was a feeling I also had during the pandemic—although, obviously, on a different scale. But that was not the end of the story.

Heavy rains followed the wildfires. Slowly, life returned. Nature, ever resilient, greened the canyons and flowers began to bloom where, not long before, there had been only charred earth.

Then one day, as I drove to the beach, millions of butterflies filled the air. I couldn't believe what I was seeing at first—it didn't seem real. I slowed the car and watched as they sailed over the windshield, never striking it.

It was a sea of butterflies, the ultimate symbol of metamorphosis.

IT WAS A SEA OF BUTTERFLIES, THE ULTIMATE SYMBOL OF METAMORPHOSIS.

When I shared this story, it resonated with people who "saw" those butterflies in their minds. It became part of their own stories— what they believe about the power of hope and the potential for transformation.

As you emotionalize your messages with stories, you can move others. People will believe and be inspired to action. That's what it's all about: inspiring others to believe, then enabling that belief to become reality.

And that, ultimately, is what it means to take control— of your own career destiny so you can lead others.

—

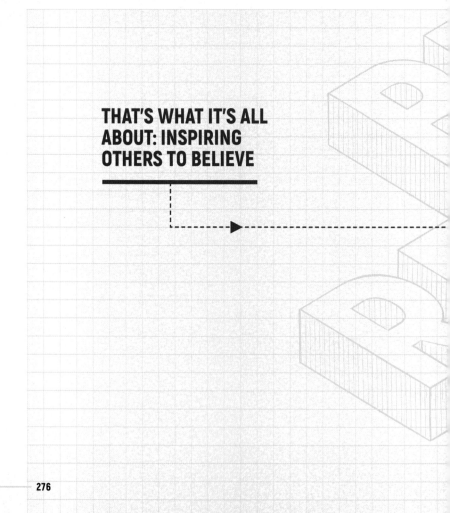

THAT'S WHAT IT'S ALL ABOUT: INSPIRING OTHERS TO BELIEVE

**THEN ENABLING
THAT BELIEF TO
BECOME REALITY**

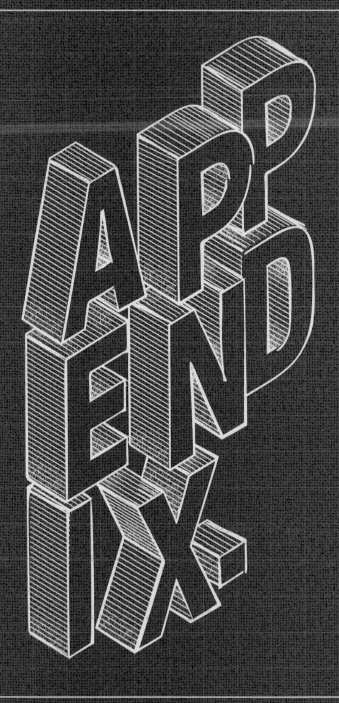

APPENDIX
RESUME EXAMPLES

To complement the discussion in Chapter 5, we've included resumes in four categories: mid-level professional, senior executive (C level), junior professional, and recent college graduate/workforce entrant.

(People, companies, and positions are hypothetical and not meant to represent real individuals or organizations. Numbers and percentages are represented by "X" to show style and format.)

Your resume is a serious document, so avoid highly stylized typefaces (like script) that distract from the business at hand.

—

THE MID-LEVEL PROFESSIONAL

The resume for Pat Sample presents an effective way to showcase competencies and experience for a mid-level professional.

Note that Pat uses a professional summary to put career and accomplishments into perspective at a glance.

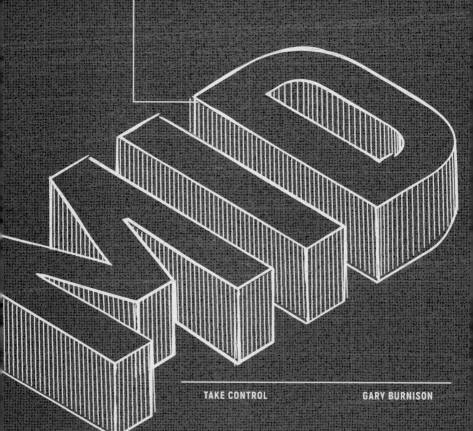

PAT SAMPLE

888 South Boulevard, Apt 2121
Phoenix, AZ, 85001
Cell (600) 600-0000 /
Home (600) 000-6600
pat.sample@sample.com

PROFESSIONAL SUMMARY

- Healthcare executive with 19 years of startup and global management consulting experience
- Deep industry expertise in payors and providers
- Experience in taking a startup from idea to profitability
- Led major strategic and operational initiatives for marquee healthcare companies

PROFESSIONAL EXPERIENCE

Health Line, Phoenix 2013–Present

Healthcare IT startup founded in 2010 by a group of Harvard alumni. Its technology platform is sold to payor organizations and enables them to compare providers using proprietary analytics.

Vice President, Product Development

- Member of the executive team, reporting to the CEO; one of the first 5 employees of the firm.
- Responsible for driving growth through the commercialization of products.

Select Achievements
- Defined client segments and economics.
- Developed data-driven sales process, resulting in XX new clients.
- Drove XX product concepts into client-ready solutions.
- Developed proprietary algorithms to support measurement of client impact.
- Formed alliances with strategic partners to further sales growth, accounting for $XX million in revenue.

Global Consulting Associates, Chicago 2009–2013

Strategy consulting group with X,XXX employees across XX offices in X countries.

Principal, Healthcare
- Led strategy, M&A, and operational improvement initiatives for leading U.S. health systems.

Select Engagements
- Program lead for the $X billion Sensar acquisition by KNT, the 3rd largest U.S. health plan. Oversaw XX teams that identified $XXX million in run-rate synergies.
- Program lead for 3-way health system merger to create a $X billion statewide network in Texas.
- Led numerous strategy and business process reengineering engagements for leading healthcare companies.

Highland Partners Consulting, Dallas 2003-2009

Boutique strategy and organizational consulting firm serving Fortune 100 clients with expertise in consumer and healthcare.

Senior Associate, Strategy Consulting (2005-2009)
- Led multi-year strategy and turnaround assignments.
- Responsibility for a team of XX consultants/associates.

Associate, Talent & Organizational Consulting (2003-2005)

EDUCATION

Harvard University
MBA, 2003

Baylor University
B.A., Economics (Honors), 2001

—

THE SENIOR EXECUTIVE

At the senior level, a professional summary becomes unnecessary because the skills and competencies that it would spotlight are expected; they are the table stakes for holding a senior-leadership position. The sample resumes for Susan and Bruce start with their professional experience, highlighting the companies they've worked for and the titles they've held.

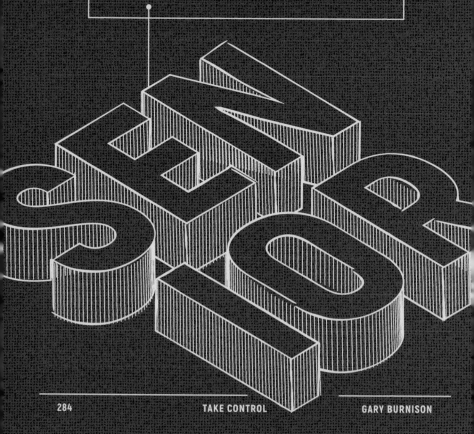

SUSAN SAMPLE

333 Garden Street
Princeton, NJ 08000
Home (222) 000-0000; Cell (333) 111-1111
Email: susan.sample@samplemail.com

PROFESSIONAL EXPERIENCE

Sentara Cosmetics, Princeton 2011–Present

High-end cosmetics company with $XXX million in revenue and X,XXX employees. At the time of hire, private-equity backed. Successful IPO in 2017.

Chief Executive Officer
- Hired by private equity firm to turn around company and accelerate growth.
- During tenure quadrupled enterprise value, grew sales by $XXX million and increased EBITDA by $XX million.

Lumeena Care, Seattle 2008–2011

Fifth largest manufacturer of personal care products in the U.S. ($XXX million in revenue and X,XXX employees). Operates as a subsidiary of The Bart Company.

Chief Marketing Officer and Head of Strategy
- Responsible for strategy, marketing, R&D, regulatory, consumer care, and M&A.
- Helped grow enterprise value by $XX million over 3 years.

Croft and Sharp, Cincinnati 2000–2008

NYSE: CAZ. Multinational personal care company with $X billion in global sales and XX,XXX employees.

Senior Vice President and General Manager, Cosmetics (2005–2008)
- Responsible for cosmetic lines with XX brands in X categories; $XXX million in sales.
- Improved annual sales growth by XX%.

Vice President, Eye Creams (2002–2005)
- Led eye creams division; increased sales and profits by X% and X%, respectively.
- Successfully launched 3 new product lines and led expansion into Latin America.

Senior Brand Manager, San Francisco (1996 -2000)
- Repositioned two major brands, increasing sales by XX%.

American Consulting Group, San Francisco (1996–2000)

Global strategy consulting firm with XX offices in XX countries.

- **Principal (1998–2000)**
  Managed all aspects of client relationships and service delivery for Fortune 500 companies with focus on retail and consumer products.

Senior Associate (1996–1998)

Nutraceuticals Productions, Los Angeles 1992–1994

Privately owned consumer goods and nutrition company with $X billion in revenue and XX,XXX employees.

Research Analyst, Marketing

EDUCATION

Cornell University
MBA, 1996

University of California Los Angeles (UCLA)
B.A. in Psychology, 1992

Boards
- Active: Board Member, WXYZ Princeton (2013–Present)
- Past: Children's Cancer Research Fund Ohio (2005–2008)

Other
- Winner "Forty under 40" (Marketing Category, 2005)
- Member of YPO (Young Presidents Organization)
- Member of the UCLA Women's Rowing Team (1989–1991)

BRUCE SAMPLE

1075 Magnolia St.
Atlanta, GA 30301
Cell: (404) 000-0000
Email: BruceSample@sample.com

PROFESSIONAL EXPERIENCE

Hogan Logistics & Transportation, Atlanta
2012–Present

Privately held intermodal logistics provider with $XXX million in annual sales and XX,XXX employees.

Chief Executive Officer (2014–Present)
- Became the first non-family CEO.
  - Delivered on growth strategy.
  - Revenue increased from $XXX million in 2014 to $XXX million in 2022.
  - EBITDA increased by XX% to $XX million.
- Successfully launched X new product lines, currently representing X% of revenue.

Chief Operating Officer (2012–2014)
- Digitized logistics infrastructure, resulting in cost savings of $XX million.
- Successfully completed a merger of equals with XYZ Logistics.

Personal Leave / Consulting 2010–2012

Took 15 months off to care for elderly parents; Continued to do consulting work for Supra Logistics.

Supra Logistics, Savannah, GA 2004–2010

Supra Logistics is $XXX million (revenue) subsidiary of Freight Forward, a UK-headquartered company

Vice President (2006–2010)

Responsible for Supra's $XXX million contract logistics business.

- Restructured business; recruited new leadership team, resulting in sales growth of XX%.

Director of Purchasing, Miami (2004–2006)

- Reengineered and executed a new strategic plan for procurement, resulting in $X million in cost savings.

Hansen Foods, Denver 1993–2004

Second largest global food/beverage company with $XXX in sales and XXX,XXX employees

Regional Foodservice Director (2001–2004)

- Led turnaround of Midwest market. Full P&L accountability for $XX million territory.

Director of Purchasing, Non-Food Category (1998–2001)

Category Manager / Senior Buyer (1995–1998)

Manager, Facility Engineering (1993–1995)

MILITARY EXPERIENCE

**United States Army, Various Worldwide Locations
1983–1993**

*Served for 10 years in a variety of leadership roles
with progressive responsibilities.*

- Executive Officer (Captain), XXX Branch.
- Aide-de-Camp for Brigadier General of XX,XXX-
  soldier logistics organization.
- Commander of transportation unit during
  Operations XYZ and ABC.
- Awarded Bronze Star.

EDUCATION

U.S. Military Academy at West Point
B.S., Economics. Graduated in top 5% of class, 1983

THE JUNIOR PROFESSIONAL

Resumes for junior professionals/executives also eliminate the professional summary, but for a reason that's entirely different from why senior executives' resumes do. Junior professionals typically do not have enough relevant experience to warrant a summary, so their resumes should instead focus immediately on their initial jobs and accomplishments.

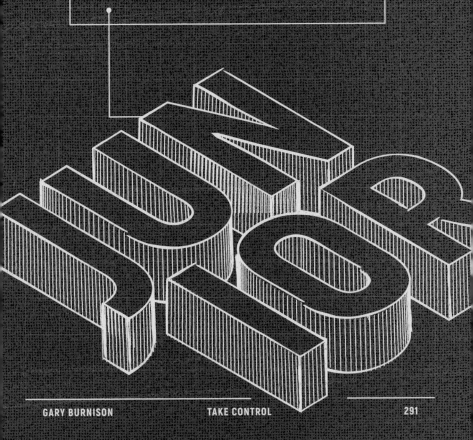

GRACE SAMPLE

111 Sunset Drive
Boston, MA 02110
Email: Grace.Sample@sample.com
Cell: (777) 111-1111

PROFESSIONAL EXPERIENCE

Raleigh Development, Boston November 2019-Present

National real estate developer with $X billion in properties.

Financial Project Manager
- Managed $XXX million of mixed-use real estate projects, from concept to completion.
- Analyzed potential real estate acquisitions across XX states, completing deals totaling $XXX million.
- Promoted to lead team of X development associates.
- Developed new valuation model that led to more than $XX million in savings for the company.

PXP Global Advisors, Boston July 2018–October 2019

Global financial advisory firm; total assets under management $X.X billion.

Associate, Private Wealth Management
- Managed client services and communication.
- Researched new investment products for partners.

EDUCATION

Lehigh University, College of Business and Economics
B.S., Business Administration, Real Estate Finance Minor, (GPA 3.9), 2018
Studied abroad at the University of Cape Town (South Africa) for 5 months (2017)

The American School in London
High School Diploma, U.S. Curriculum, 2013

ACTIVITIES AND ORGANIZATIONS

Lehigh University CBE Study Abroad Mentor Program
Co-founder and vice president; one of two students selected to start the CBE Study Abroad Mentor Program.

Lehigh University Basketball Club
Treasurer

Kappa Alpha Society, Pennsylvania Alpha Chapter
President

SKILLS

Series 66, Project Management Professional (PMP) Certification

LEE SAMPLE

111 Everest Drive, Apt # 222
Arlington, VA 55555
Email: lsample@leesamplefashion.com
Cell: 411-000-0000

SOCIAL MEDIA:

Twitter: @LeeSampleFashion
Instagram: LeeSampleFashion
Personal Website: http://leesample.aboutme
LinkedIn: https://www.linkedin.com/in/leesample

PROFESSIONAL EXPERIENCE

Lee Sample Fashion, LLC, Arlington, VA
2020–Present

Online fashion brand with annual sales of $X million and XX employees. www.leesamplefashion.com

Co-Founder and CEO
- Developed worldwide fashion brand with XX,XXX Instagram and Twitter followers.
- Media and celebrity endorsements, including Viva, Glama, and ABCD.
- Closed XX partnerships with companies in the U.S., U.K., India, and Japan.
- Company in process of being acquired by a leading global fashion house (expected close of sale end of 2022).

Personal Gap Year 2014

Traveled to XX countries across Europe and Asia.

Dimension Brands, Washington, D.C. June–December 2018

Leading advertising and branding firm.

Junior Brand Manager
- Launched social media activities for Dimension Brands.

Internships

Keisuki Fashion, New York
Intern, Summer of 2017

Donald Investment Management, Baltimore
Summer intern, 2015 and 2016 (3 months each)

EDUCATION

Johns Hopkins University
B.A., Economics, Minor in Engineering 2018

SKILLS

Fluent in Mandarin (speaking and writing)

RECENT COLLEGE GRADUATE

Recent college graduates/workforce entrants' resumes typically start with their education and degrees. Work experience and internships are listed separately to clearly differentiate paid from non-paid work experience.

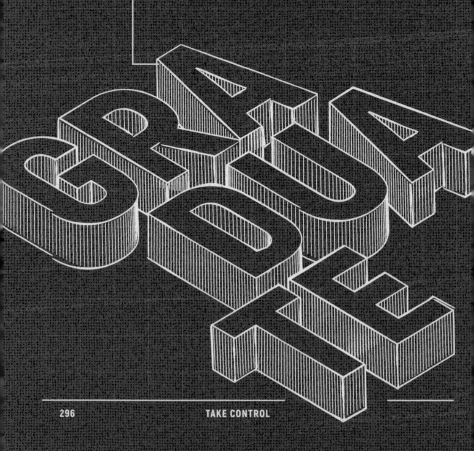

STEPHANIE SAMPLE

123 W. 112 St.
New York, NY 12312
Cell: 212-111-1111
Stephanie.sample@sample.com
www.stephanie.sample.net

EDUCATION

Syracuse University
B.A. in Communications, Minor in Political Science
2021 (GPA 4.0)
Academic Honors Summa Cum Laude, Dean's List
(2020, 2021)

WORK EXPERIENCE

NewPost.com, New York October 2021–Present
*Digital news site averaging XXX million page views
per month.*

Editorial Assistant – Political Desk
Part of editorial team covering state politics. Work
closely with managing editor, participating in daily news
meetings. Manage home page for NewPost/NY.com
website, coordinating social media and monitoring traffic.

INTERNSHIPS

HallinganPolitics.com, New York June–October 2021

Popular political news blog (owned by Big Media LLC).

Editorial Intern
- Assisted in all facets of news reporting, writing, and editing, including for award-winning SpotCheck investigative team.

WNNY, Syracuse January–May 2021

Local XYZ News affiliate station.

Production Intern
- Assisted production team; worked on WNNY.com website.

Relevant Skills and Extracurricular Activities
Proficient in Spanish; Spent two summers (2019 and 2020) with America Serves Student Volunteers in infant/mother wellness program in Dominican Republic.

President of Beta Gamma Beta Sorority 2021